KA LEI

THE LEIS OF HAWAII

MARIE A. MCDONALD
Photographs and Illustrations by ROEN MCDONALD
TOPGALLANT PUBLISHING CO., LTD.
Second Printing

Wearing Leis

NO KA'OHINANI

Making a Lei

Second printing 1981
First printing 1978

TOPGALLANT PUBLISHING CO., LTD.
845 Mission Lane
Honolulu, Hawaii 96813

Typeset in the United States of America
Printed in Taiwan

Library of Congress Cataloging in Publication Data applied for:

McDonald, Marie.
Ka lei

1. McDonald, Marie______

ISBN 0-914916-32-7 (paper)
ISBN 0-914916-33-5 (cloth)

Giving a Lei

ACKNOWLEDGMENTS

This book is the result of many years of seeking information through questioning, listening, reading, and experimenting. There is not space enough to list all who aided in the seeking, who heard my questions, and to whom I listened, nevertheless, to all who helped, my sincere appreciation is expressed here. Mahalo nui loa.

I am indebted to Beatrice Krauss whose encouragement and support in the preparation of this book was limitless; Anita Won who typed and re-typed the text with patience and matchless skill; Larry Kimura who checked the manuscript for clarity and correctness of Hawaiian terms and words; Derral Herbst who checked the manuscript for clarity and correctness of biological information and made many suggestions to improve the text; Allison Kay who checked the lists of shells; and others listed here who contributed information, helped to find plants, and allowed us to photograph items from their collections:

Betsy Harrison Gagne
Mary Kawena Pukui
Nora Potter
Herbert Shipman
Lester W. "Bill' Bryan
William and Elizabeth Ahia
Scott Seymour
Harry Joao
Edwina Noelani Mahoe
R. Alex Anderson
Betty Lou Ho
Etelka Mahoe Adams
Clara Nākī Brito
Irma and Walter Pomroy
Lydia K. Aholo
Mary Bell
Hannah Lekelesa
Nancy Fuller
Annette and John Ka'ohelauli'i
Evelyn Kahale
John Kauwe
Alice Namakelua

Paul R. Weissich—Honolulu Botanical Gardens, City and County of Honolulu.

'Āina K. Keawe, Shigeru Naramoto, Adeline Maunapau Lee—Hawaiiana Center, Department of Parks and Recreation, City and County of Honolulu.

George Nozawa and Herbert Kikukawa—Forestry Division, Department of Land and Natural Resources, State of Hawaii.

Many thanks to those who allowed us to photograph items from their collections: Florence Chang, seed leis; Betsy Harrison Gagne, Ni'ihau shell leis; Mary Ann Bigelow, shell, feather and other leis; John Spencer and Eunice He-a, lei palaoa; Frank Cook, lei palaoa and feather leis; Billie Strauss, feather and shell leis; and Mr. and Mrs. Albert Solomon, Kamuela Museum, paper leis.

I am especially grateful for the help given to me by Lee and Kepā Maly who assisted with the index and Henry Geis who completed the photographic work and John I. Kjargaard.

Mahalo nui loa me ke aloha to my husband, Bill, and my children, Roen, Susan and David who helped by always being kind and thoughtful.

Any omissions or errors in this book are not the fault of those who helped me.

Receiving a Lei

Enjoying a Lei

TABLE OF CONTENTS

LEIS OF THE POLYNESIAN PERIOD

Hala leis: Hawai'i, Tonga and Samoa (left to right)

From the very beginning, it seemed that there was a lei to mark the most memorable moments of my life—not just the joyous and happy moments, but also those that were filled with sadness and grief, the times of anticipation and nostalgia, the occasions of accomplishment and pride, the antagonizing periods of questioning and the exciting moments of discovery. The lei was there to mark the beginning of my life. It was in my name. And when thought and reason became a part of me, I wondered: Is it true, the story I used to hear the tūtū ladies tell? "Be careful what you name your child—she will live up to it," they would say, then elaborate with examples, most of which were rather mysterious with unhappy outcomes. Is it true?

I laughed and played, romped in the sun, hiked in the mountains, bounced on horseback, swam in sweet, icy cold, fresh water pools and warm Pacific blue waters with a lei as a companion. I have given with admiration and honor, a lei. Sometimes in the giving, I've wept with grief and sometimes in the giving, the weeping was joyful. There was a time when nostalgia and longing for the familiar was kindled in the depth of me because there was a withered up lei far from the shores of home.

I have given and received a lei of adolescent love, a lei of true love, and a lei of parental love. I've sent a lei half way around the world to remind someone that there was still love. I've said hello and goodbye with a lei. I've lain lei after lei upon the tombs of Hawai'i's kings and queens. I've danced with leis encircling my head and neck, and both wrists and ankles. I've made a lei, many leis, and I've taught my children and many others to make them.

And, in my best alto voice accompanied by ukuleles, guitars, bongo drums, good friends and relatives made mellow by much food and cold beer, I've sung the praises to the lei . . . "lei 'awapuhi, lei hiki ahiahi" . . . "Sweet lei mamo (mamo), lei o ke aloha (aloha)" . . . "A he lei mau no ku'u kino."

Then, because of the lei, I've begun to discover what was my mother's and her forebearers', what is mine and what will be my children's heritage.

In every part of the world where man has lived and lives, he has made for himself a lei, a necklace, a crown of various materials to adorn his body, to ward off evil spirits, to bring good fortune, to please his gods, to denote rank among men, to give as tokens of love, and for pure and simple enjoyment. The materials, colors, the arrangements, the textures, the techniques, yes, even the lasting quality, the mobility and scent of the materials fascinated him. It is true that these leis have a common character, but it is also true that the common character was enhanced by each culture that produce them. Man's need for such embellishment, the availability of materials and the limitations of technique has produced differences of style with each culture. The general common character and similarities in details between the Hawaiian lei and those occurring in other parts of the world suggest an actual common origin of people who made them, or, at least that communication existed between the cultures involved, no matter how far apart in space and time they may have been.

Man from the earliest of times adorned himself with some kind of lei. In his primitive beginnings he could not have been completely devoid of emotional and aesthetic reaction and interaction with his natural surroundings. He could not have reacted just for the sake of survival alone and not have been aware of the sights, scents, sounds and "feels" of nature without wanting to collect parts of it, to put together these parts, and to carry them around with him as prized possessions, or symbols of magic. What better place to carry them than around the neck or head, leaving arms and legs free and unencumbered to do the work of survival.

The very first necklaces and crowns were probably made of perishable, natural materials, flowers, leaves and fruits. This we can safely assume since early man was a forest dwelling creature. Evidences of the very first leis have not lasted through the eons of time, however, others of more lasting materials of the same Paleolithic period have survived. These leis of bone, ivory, shells, animal teeth, and even fish bones have been unearthed in graves, caves and in other places where early man has lived. These crude necklaces of non-perishable materials were replaced by hand-tooled beaded necklaces of Neolithic man. Beads and pendants carved from soft stone, ivory, or fashioned from glass or clay have been discovered in the ruins of the Neolithic civilizations of the Indus Valley, China, Mesopotamia, and Egypt (3500–200 B.C.).

Each succeeding civilization-culture the world over had its leis. The Aztecs and Mayans had their leis of gold and feathers and, most probably, their leis of flowers, leaves and fruits. In pre-Christian times, the people who inhabited the great and small land masses of the earth all seemed to have some kind of lei, some perishable and some nonperishable. Some of the nonperishable ones have been unearthed by archaeologists, thus verifying their existence in those early times. The perishable ones have long disintegrated. Only threads of information remain, but these threads lead us to believe that certainly the perishable leis did exist.

Europeans of pre-Christian times wove garlands of flowers and ferns in celebration of pagan rites for heralding the coming of spring. The earliest recorded perishable leis are the Greek crowns of laurel and olive (c. 750 B.C.).

The *Laurus nobilis* was sacred to Apollo. Its leaves were woven into a lei and was used by the Greeks to crown their heroes and to mark men of distinctively high office. Later, the crown of laurel was used to indicate academic honors. The practice of wearing the laurel lei as a mark of distinction was continued by the Romans and Byzantines.

The olive (*Olea europaea*), the Greek sign of peace and Minerva's gift to man, was used to deck the victors in the Olympic games. Modern man still uses the laurel and the olive to crown heroes, to mark men of distinction and to denote peace.

Christ was crowned with a lei of thorns. Although there is a legend that tells us that this lei was fashioned from branches of a plant called "crown of thorns," *Euphorbia milii* var. *splendens,* it seems unlikely since this plant is native to Madagascar and there are many, many thorny plants of the biblical area which could have served this purpose well.

In Asia, Hindus made leis of jasmine, and Buddhists made chains of beads made from the wood of the orange champak tree, while Malaysians used the fragrant flowers for garlands. The Chinese crafted leis of jade, pearls, and gold. The Melanesians, the Africans, the American Indians made necklaces and crowns of bark, feathers, shells, ivory, clay, wood and metal. Royal heads of Europe created ornate crowns of precious jewels. In every part of the world where man has lived and lives, he has made himself a lei.

It is believed that the Hawaiian Islands were populated by people who came from southern Asia, after many hundreds of years of migrating from island to island eastward across the vast Pacific Ocean, intermingling in the course of this migration with peoples of other racial strains. These people may have been forced from their lands by political or economic wars, or they may have been blown off course by storms, or they may have been compelled to migrate because of man's insatiable urge to explore the unknown. Whatever the reason, scholars agree that some of these migrating people finally reached Hawai'i about 750 A.D. They also agree that the first settlers came from the Marquesas, some two thousand miles to the south of Hawai'i.

In the Twelfth Century, invaders from Tahiti came. They gave to the islands the name, Hawaiki, the ancient name of Raiatea from which they came. Other Tahitians followed. Travel between the Society and Hawaiian Islands continued through the Fourteenth Century. The invaders brought with them their favorite and necessary possessions, their culture and fond memories of the lands that they left behind.

Among the necessary and favorite possessions, the culture, and fond memories of the lands that they left behind, the settlers brought with them the art and traditions of the lei which generations before them had developed on the continent of their origin. If the original materials of their ancestral leis were not available, they substituted materials that resembled the original. The reasons for and the rituals of the lei suffered changes also as peoples moved from place to place, materials and techniques changed, sociological, physical and spiritual needs changed.

The leis of the settlement period in Hawaiian history were really Polynesian. They resembled those that were found in other parts of Polynesia. They, like other artifacts of times gone by, help tell the story of man's existence in time and space.

Such temporary fragrant leis as maile and hala, and such nonperishable leis as the early forms of lei niho palaoa, lei pūpū, and lei hulu manu appear throughout Polynesia and the Pacific basin. The lei of green elliptical fragrant leaves is probably the oldest of all leis. The idea started on the Asian continent and as people migrated west to the Mediterranean region and north to the temperate zone, and east to Malaya to the easternmost part of Polynesia, and from the Society Islands to Hawai'i, they took with them the lei itself or the idea of this lei. In the Mediterranean, the lei was made of laurel. In some parts of Polynesia, the lei was fashioned with the leaves of *Alyxia stellata*. In Hawai'i, the bark and leaves of the maile, *Alyxia olivaeformis*, was used. The original idea is probably lost to the ages, however, the outgrowths still thrive.

The lei hala, necklace of keys from the pandanus fruit, was found throughout Polynesia and Micronesia. The plant was probably carried by the settlers of the great Pacific basin as they moved from southern Asia, south to New Zealand and Australia, east and north to Hawai'i. The style and the design of the lei differs with each group of people that made it. In Samoa, the entire key of the fruit was strung through the fibrous or nut end, crosswise and at an angle, creating a chevron pattern. In Tonga, slivers from the fibrous end of the key were attached to leaves. In Hawai'i, the fibrous end of the key was cut free of the nut end and strung lengthwise through the center.

The kinds of leis that the early Hawaiians made and used will help to substantiate their migratory patterns in pre-historical times, just as they are helping to tell the story of those people who settled in Hawai'i after the islands were discovered by Captain Cook.

Travel between Hawai'i and the islands to the south ceased by the end of the Fourteenth Century. Hawai'i was isolated from the rest of the world until the arrival of Captain Cook in January, 1778. During this period of isolation, the Hawaiians developed a culture free of outside contacts, influenced only by the memories of those that preceded them. They built upon these memories, culled, refined and polished them until they established for themselves a sophisticated "primitive" culture. Primitive by modern standards only because there was no written language and there existed no metals within their environment, and the people had to rely on stone implements to create their arts and crafts, their architecture, to farm, to build their canoes, to fashion their musical instruments, to wage war. Sophisticated in that they developed a refined social and political structure consisting of kinship groups, hereditary leaders, priests, nobles, scholars, commoners, and a class without rights. They were capable of logical, rational thought and action. Religious practices were based on their belief in the supernatural force, "mana", about which they set up a cult of gods and heroes.

One important cultural characteristic of this time was the nonsegmented lifestyle of the Hawaiian. Life was not segregated into specialized areas as it is in highly advanced civilizations. One area of living overlapped other areas, creating a fused way of life. Politics, religion, recreation, education, medicine, the arts, agriculture, navigation, and all else were not divided into separate units of living, but were so closely related that it is difficult for present day observers and students of Hawaiiana to make definite judgments as to whether a specific act was wholly religious or simply a necessity, or whether another act was the result of a belief in the supernatural or just a means to an end.

The lei, like this important cultural characteristic, was not subjected to separate pockets of living. It appeared in the fields with the farmer when he invoked the blessing of the gods upon his fields and crops; it was a necessary ornament for the dancer; it was worn by the nursing mother; it was used in the healing rites of the kahuna lapa'au, the healing priest. It was the mark of chiefly rank. It was offered to the gods. It was a symbol of love and lovemaking. It belonged to the festivals and it brightened up the routine of daily life as well. Children made them. Men and women made them. Gods and goddesses favored them. The poets sang their praises.

A greater and richer variety of leis was made in Hawai'i at this time than in any other Polynesian group. Some of the leis were of a more permanent nature while others were made only to endure a short period of time. While the permanent leis were valued for their permanency, the temporary ones were equally valued for the short time that they existed. The beauty of each type was no less beautiful than the other. They were valued more for what they represented.

LEI PALAOA, LEI NIHO PALAOA, LEI HOAKA, AND LEI NIHO 'ĪLIO
(Ivory, Tusk And Teeth Leis)

The permanent leis included those that were made of such materials as feathers, shells, seeds, ivory, and teeth of various animals. Those of feathers and ivory ornamented the bodies of the ali'i or the ruling class and the kahuna or learned class.

I wish now that when I first saw this awesome lei niho palaoa, it would have been tied about the neck of a resolute, proud, regal, tight muscled Hawaiian male of thirty years or so, but this was not, and never to be. I first saw this lei in a poorly lighted, cold, impersonal, museum show case. I was fourteen years old and my immediate reaction to it after reading the label was "ugh." I had formed a prejudice. I did not know it. I did not understand its reason for being and at the time, I did not care.

Some years later, in preparation for a storytelling session with Honolulu playground children, I read the story of 'Umi and His Royal Necklace and as if it were the first dawn of all times, I realized that something had been totally lacking in my education. I knew the tales of Hans Christian Andersen. I had read the Anglo-Saxon epic of Beowulf. I studied the effects of the American and Russian Revolutions and researched Roman and Byzantine art. I knew all about apple trees and how they got to Pennsylvania and Ohio, but at no time during the course of being educated had I heard the story of 'Umi and His Royal Necklace. Most alarming was the fact that I was twenty-two years old, of half Hawaiian ancestry with four years of college tucked under my belt, and I did not know this story and many more stories that had come out of my environment and my hereditary past.

I read more, listened more, searched more, and studied more. Then, I understood more and appreciated more the legacy that was always mine.

The most spectacular of the permanent leis was the lei niho palaoa or lei palaoa. According to Te Rangi Hiroa (Peter H. Buck) in Arts and Crafts of Hawai'i, the lei niho palaoa, hook-shaped pendant carved from a sperm whale's tooth and attached to coils of finely braided human hair, replaced an earlier model found in the Marquesas, Mangareva, the Catham Islands, early New Zealand, and in early Hawai'i. The prototypes, lei 'ōpu'u, were uncarved, whole sperm whale teeth pendants and copies of them made from wood and stone. The carved hook-shaped pendant suspended on coils of human hair appear only in Hawai'i.

Te Rangi Hiroa further described the various lei palaoa that are contained in the Bishop Museum collection and details the method of constructing them. It is recommended that his descriptions and details be read.

Most of the hook-shaped ivory pendants were about three to five inches in length. Some were as small as an inch in length, while others were as long as six and a half inches. The pendant consisted of an irregular shank which curved into a hook or tongue at the lower end. Sometimes the ivory pendant was dyed yellow by smoking it over burning red sugar cane. A hole was drilled from side to side through the lower end of the shank. Many coils of human hair, sometimes numbering well over a thousand, were passed through or attached to the holes at either side of the shank. (see illustration, plates 1, 2, 3 page 6, 7, 8).

The construction of the coils of human hair which supported the pendant was complicated. The bulk of the eight ply braided coils were not passed through the hole in the shank. A few long coils of about twelve to eighteen inches in length were first passed through the shank hole (a and b). Then, many more shorter coils of half the length of the long coils were attached to either side of the pendant with an olonā tying cord (c). The tying cord circled the lower loops of the coils on one side, passed through the shank hole, and circled the lower loops of the coils of the other side (d.) The circling and passing through was repeated several times. The coils were then drawn up tightly against the sides of the shank. The knots and ends of the tying cord were concealed by the longer coils which were then spread out evenly surrounding and covering the shorter ones.

The coils were drawn up evenly, were bunched together and tied with a binding cord an inch or two from their ends. Threads of olonā were passed through the upper loops of the inner coils. A long, single strand of braided hair or olonā was wound around the threads and through the remaining loops of the outer coils and was drawn up with the binding cord to form the core of the neck cord. The fine threads of olonā were divided into eight strands and were braided around the core of the neck cord (e, f, g). The neck cords were about eight to ten inches long on each side.

The lei palaoa, a war club, and a loin cloth served as identification of kinship of 'Umi, son of Liloa. King Liloa of Waipi'o, while on a trip, met and took for his wife the beautiful

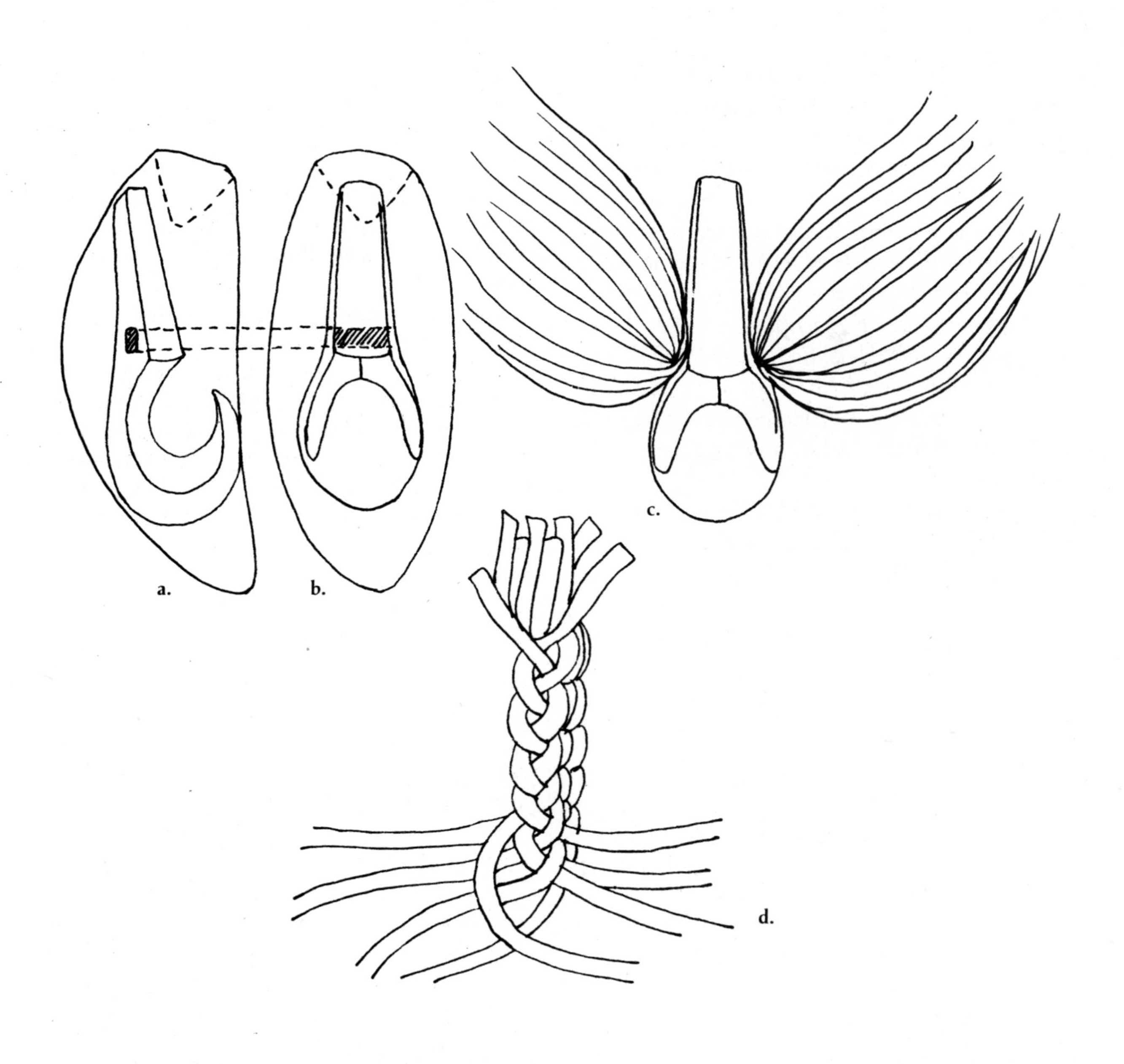

PLATE 1. LEI PALAOA. CUTTING THE PENDANT AND PLAITING THE LOOPS.
a. Side view: placement of pendant design on sperm whale tooth
b. front view
c. completed pendant
d. square, eight-strand plait

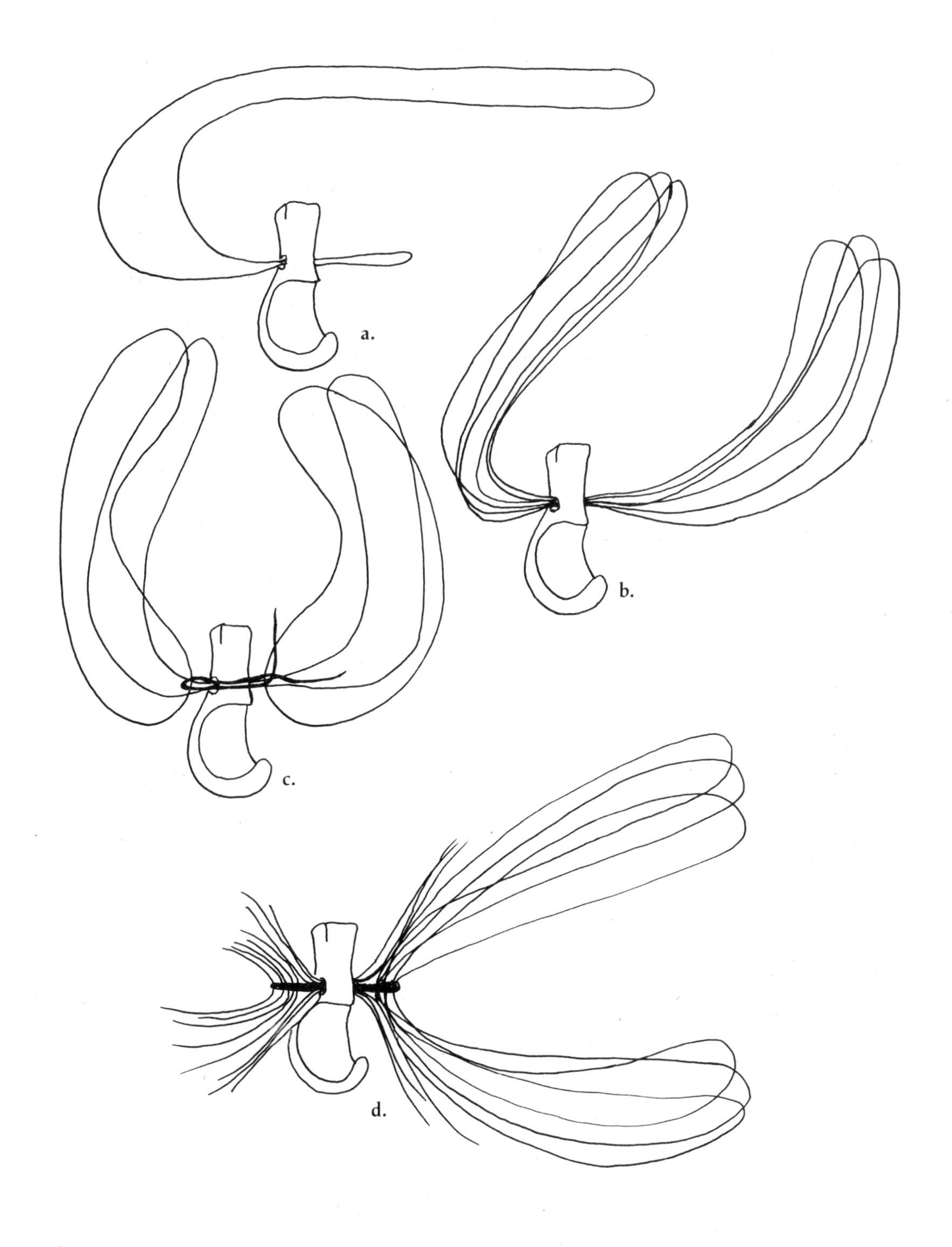

PLATE 2. LEI PALAOA. ATTACHING THE SUSPENSION COILS TO THE PENDANT.

a, b, threading the long continuous loops through the shank hole

c. attaching shorter loops to the sides of the pendant

d. securing the shorter loops with an olonā tie and spreading out the longer ones to cover the construction ties and knots

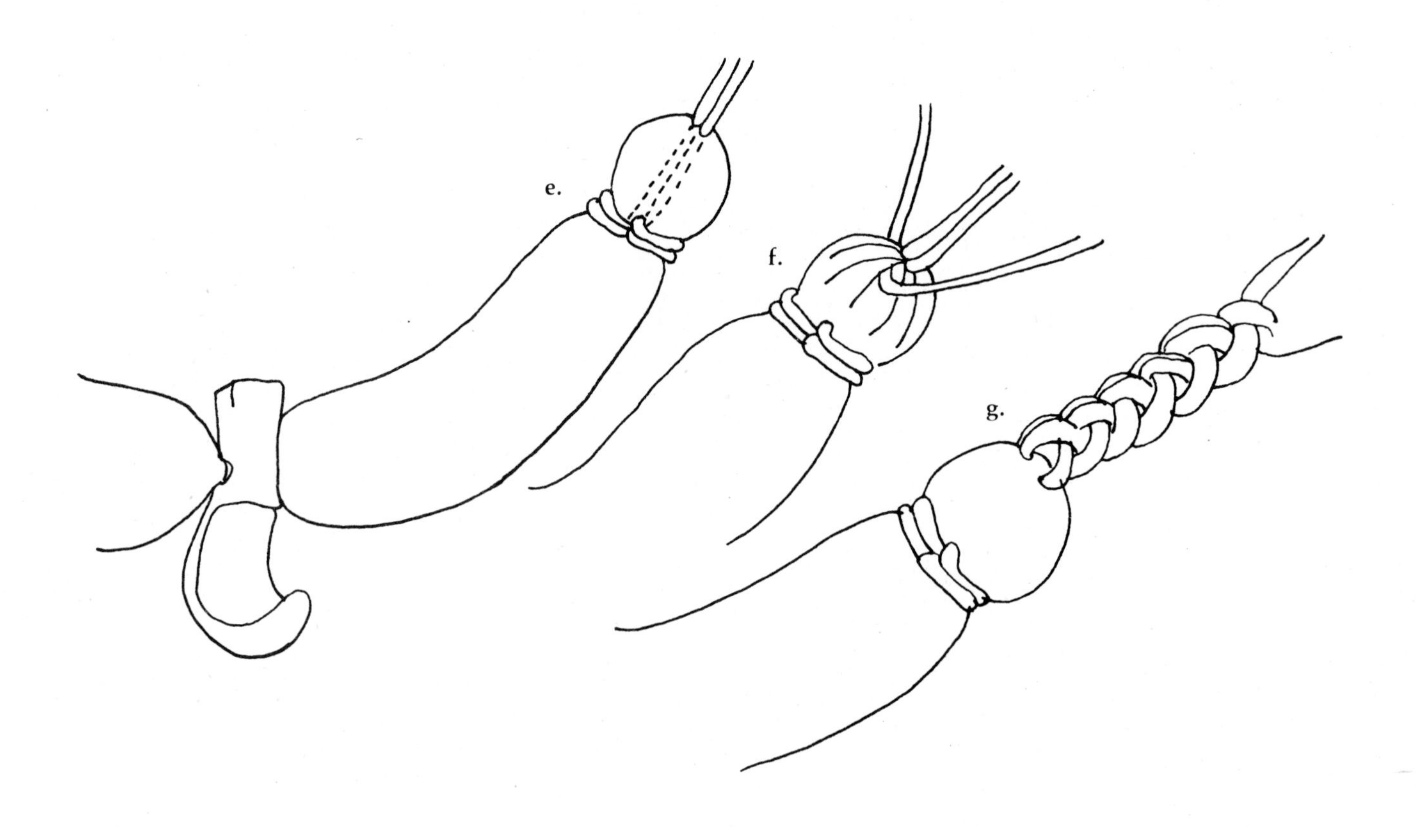

PLATE 3. LEI PALAOA. COMPLETING THE LEI.

a. passing the olonā cord around and through coil ends
b. passing olonā threads through upper ends of loops until loop ends are all caught up
c. plaiting the neck cord

Akahiakuleana. When it became apparent that Akahiakuleana was with child, Liloa left her to return to his family in Waipi'o. Upon leaving, he told her to name the child after her family if it should be a girl, but if it should be a boy, she should call him 'Umi. Akahiakuleana asked the king how he would know that the boy child was his. Liloa replied by giving her three tokens—his lei palaoa, his loin cloth, and his war club. "When it is full grown give these to the child as his," Liloa said and left.

Akahiakuleana had a boy child and she called him 'Umi as she was directed. When the boy had grown, Akahiakuleana sent him to Waipi'o girdled in the loin cloth of Liloa, with the lei palaoa about his neck, and a servant, Omaokamau, carrying the war club, to search out his father. 'Umi's mother cautioned him to take care, directed him to enter the back door of Liloa's house and when he found Liloa, he was to sit on his lap. Show him the tokens of kinship and when he asks for your name, tell him that you are 'Umi.

'Umi went to Waipi'o with Omaokamau and his friend, Pi'imaiwa'a. He found his father and displayed the tokens of kinship. Liloa accepted him as his son and told all of his people.

It was one of these tokens of kinship, the lei palaoa, which in later years led to a war between the district of Hāmākua and Hilo.

When 'Umi-a Liloa became chief of Hāmākua, he had taken for his wife the daughter of Kulukulua, chief of Hilo. On one occasion during his stay in Hilo, he attended a grand party where there was much dancing and many games. On this occasion, he noticed that the daughter of Kulukulua was wearing around her head and about her shoulders leis of feathers and a necklace with a hook-shaped wiliwili *(Erythrina sandwicensis)* wood pendant. It was the wiliwili ornament which attracted his attention and he asked the princess if this was her royal necklace. It was.

'Umi ridiculed the Hilo symbol of royalty saying that where he came from this ornament was worn by anyone who chose to do so. The necklace of his chiefs was made of finely woven cords of human hair to which was attached a hook-like pendant cut from a whale's tooth. As he ridiculed, he snatched the necklace from about the princess' neck and broke it.

The princess was heartbroken. She told Kulukulua, her father, of the broken necklace and the necklace of 'Umi-a-Liloa. This angered the chief. He ordered 'Umi and his companions, all save one, bound! He gave the spared companion, Pi'imaiwa'a, one day to produce the necklace of human hair and whale ivory. If the command was not carried out, 'Umi and the remaining companions would be put to death.

Pi'imaiwa'a hurried to Waipi'o and returned with the sacred necklace of 'Umi's royal father Liloa. The necklace was given to Kulukulua. 'Umi was released. He prayed for the safekeeping of the necklace until he could return to reclaim it.

'Umi returned to Waipi'o and immediately planned for his campaign to reclaim the necklace.

Many men were killed in the campaign. 'Umi was victorious. The royal insignia of the House of Liloa was returned to Waipi'o. Hilo and Hāmākua were united with 'Umi as king.

The lei niho palaoa is spectacular to behold. It is even more spectacular when one realizes that its function was more than ornamentation. It was fashioned from love and honor, worn as a mark of social rank, and passed on to bind one generation to another, and still another to insure one's heritage and one's all important family ties. It is believed that the tongue shaped pendant represented the authority of the ruling class. The women wore the lei palaoa with large hooks while the men wore those with smaller hooks.

After whalers, adventurers and seamen introduced to Hawai'i the tools and materials of their civilization, the lei palaoa took on a new dimension. The suspension coils of human hair were replaced by ivory beads. The hook-shaped pendant remained the same, with the exception of its crafting. Walrus tusks were used and the carving and drilling was done with metal tools rather than stone tools. The restrictive use by the ali'i class was still perpetuated.

With the death of Kamehameha the First, the coming of more haoles, foreigners, and the overthrow of the ancient Hawaiian systems of government, society, and religion, the ruling classes lost interest in their royal insignia. They were dazzled by the jewels, beads, and baubles of the foreigners. The lei palaoa gave way to the necklaces of western man. Many were given or exchanged and are now parts of collections of museums the world over. Few remain with the Hawaiian families. Few monarchs after Kamehameha I even wore the lei palaoa on state occasions.

Ivory from other animals were used for necklaces and bracelets also. Boar's tusks were polished and holes drilled in the base ends, and strung on olonā cord. Many tusks, sometimes spaced with smaller pieces (beads) of tusks or shells, were used to form a short, tight fitting necklace called lei hoaka, or a single tusk was extended on a length of cord.

The lei niho 'īlio was made with dogs' canine teeth which were pierced and strung on lengths of cord. Some were believed to be permanent leis. The dog's teeth in these leis were spaced with shells. Most of the other lei niho 'īlio were believed to be just a convenient and safe way to store the teeth for use later in ankle ornaments called, kūpe'e niho 'īlio.

LEI HULU MANU
(Feather Leis)

Since great value was placed on feathers for garments by the ali'i who vied to outdo each other with various colored patterns, a guild of professional bird catchers called po'e kahai manu, was established. Guild members caught some of the birds with a sticky substance from the fruit of the pāpala kēpau *(Pisonia)*, others they snared or stoned. Some birds were released after the needed feathers were removed. Others were eaten.

Yellow feathers were of greater value than red. Black and green feathers were the least desired. Feathers, as well as other things of value, were collected by the konohiki, tax collectors, who circled the islands during the time of the makahiki, the festival honoring Lono, god of all growing things, as payment to the ali'i.

Small, native, forest dwelling, honeycreepers were chief providers of feathers for leis. The deep yellow feathers of the mamo, *(Drepanis pacifica)*, was the most valuable since only a few feathers from the upper and under side of the tail and on the thighs were yellow. Most important, the bird was only found on the island of Hawai'i. The lighter yellow feathers of the 'ō'ō, *(Moho nobilis)*, ranked second in value. Like the mamo, only a few tufts of yellow feathers from an otherwise black bird could be used. The 'ō'ō, however, was found in the forests of all the islands. The 'i'iwi, *(Vestiaria coccinea)*, and the 'apapane, *(Himatione sanguinea)*, provided red feathers. The latter, a darker red. The 'ō'ū. *(Psittirostra psittacea)*, provided the green feathers. Black feathers were taken from the mamo and 'ō'ō. Black and green feathers were used only as contrast and very seldom, if ever, as the only color in a lei.

Only male members of the feather craft guild were allowed to make the feather garments of the chiefs. The lei hulu manu, however, were made by both men and women. The men caught the birds, the women sorted the feathers.

As it is with the making of most leis, the gathering and preparation of the materials took more time than the actual making of the lei. Feather leis probably involve more time and painstaking work than any other kind of lei. This, coupled with the facts that the feathers were very small and that many were needed, and that they were not very easy to acquire, that they were of a lasting and sensuous quality, made the lei hulu manu valuable.

The feathers were sorted into various like sizes and colors, and stored in pandanus or kapa packages. When enough feathers were acquired, the leis were made. Small bunches of feathers were attached to a center cord of coconut husk or olonā, *(Touchardia latifolia)*, with a binding thread of banana, hau, or olonā fiber. The bunch consisted of one large feather and several small ones. Sometimes the lei maker changed the color of some of the small feathers in the bunches, as in the case of many lei mamo and lei 'ō'ō, to make the overall color appear deeper. As each bunch was placed on the center cord, the binding thread was passed over the quill end of the feathers several times and secured in place with a half hitch knot. Successive bunches were added until the entire circumference and length of the cord was covered. The bunches of feathers were not individually tied together before the binding process took place.

The feather bunches were put together with individual feathers all turning the same way, that is, underside (concave curve) to topside (convex curve) of the feather. The bunches were placed on the center cord, again, with the feathers all turning the same way. Some leis had alternate sections of feathers curving away from the center cord and feathers curving toward the center cord. (see illustration, plate 4, a, b, c, Page 12).

Leis of one single color were more valuable than those of two or more colors. Yellow feather leis were more valuable than the other colors. Feather leis were usually identified by the feathers that were used: lei mamo, lei 'ō'ō, lei 'i'iwi, lei 'apapane. A lei of mixed feathers in varying lengths and colors was called lei piki. (see illustration, plate 4, c, page 12). A lei with spiral designs of various colors was called lei pāni'o; one with sections of various colors, lei paukū, lei paukūkū, or lei pāwehe; and one with feathers turning toward the center cord, lei kāmoe. These names are often applied to leis of other materials also.

The lei hulu manu was the most valuable possession of the women of the ali'i class. These leis she wore proudly about her head and neck to denote her rank.

The lei hulu manu also decorated the bamboo and tapa standard of the makahiki image of the god, Lono, and the masts of the ocean going canoes to show wind direction.

As new birds were introduced to Hawai'i, the feathers were tested for their lei making qualities. The Hawaiians, eventually, used the feathers from pheasants (kolohala), pea fowls (pīkake), ducks (kakā), gooney birds (kone), guinea fowls (kini), quails (manu-kapalulu), chickens (moa), and others. Instead of securing these feathers to a center cord by winding a thread around them and the cord, as was done in the earlier lei hulu, they secured the feathers to a foundation of cotton or silk fabric by sewing each feather in place with two or more overcast stitches using needle and thread. These feather leis are worn with pride by both men and women of contemporary times usually as bands about their hats.

The introduction of new plant and animal life to Hawai'i upset the ecological balance, causing the near extinction of the native mamo, 'ō'ō, 'i'iwi, 'apapane, 'ō'ū and others. Today, the lei hulu manu of old Hawai'i is rarely seen unless it is in museums the world over, in private collections, or on occasions when Hawaiians gather to celebrate a special event.

LEI PŪPŪ
(Shell Leis)

The beaches, reefs, and even the valleys and mountains were the sources for the pūpū,

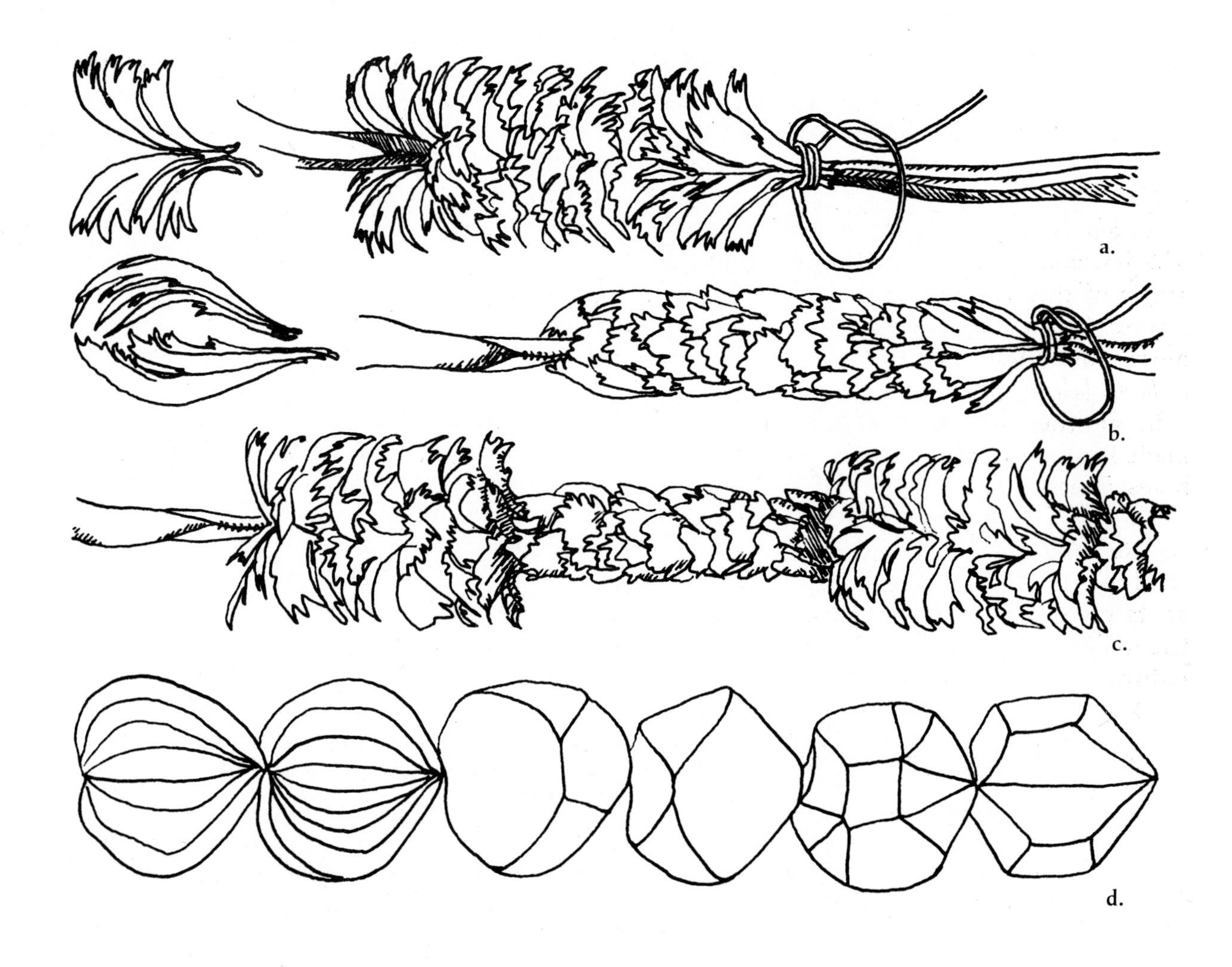

PLATE 4. LEI HULU MANU AND LEI KUKUI.

a. **Securing feathers to the central cord. Bunches of feathers arranged curving** away from the cord
b. Lei kāmoe: bunches of feathers arranged curving toward the cord
c. Lei piki: a combination of bunches of feathers curving toward and away from the cord
d. Lei kukui containing nuts with various textures, facets and patterns

shells of the lei maker. Small and medium sized shells were strung on lengths of fine olonā cord. The technique was very simple. In one method, the cord was passed through the natural openings, apertures, in the shells and was held in place with a stuffing of soft fibers. The lei leho, cowrie shell necklace, is an example of this method. Various cowries were strung in this manner: *Cypraea moneta,* the most commonly used cowrie, *C. isabella, C. carneola, C. helvola,* and *C. poraria.*

In another method, artificial holes were made in the shells to facilitate stringing. The holes were drilled, filed down and or punctured out. In the lei pipipi (*Nerita picea* and *N. neglecta*) and lei kūpe'e *(N. polita),* the artificial holes were made by filing down the high spots on the whorl, then punching through them. Each shell was then strung through the natural aperture and the punched out hole.

The most highly prized shell necklaces were the lei pūpū o Ni'ihau, the momi *(Euplica varians)* and the kahele-lani *(Leptothyra verruca).* Shells were gathered from the beaches on the western shores of Ni'ihau and Kaua'i. The spire on each shell was filed down to create a hole for stringing. The shells were strung through their apertures and the filed down hole. Often the shells were gathered with the spires already filed down by sand and wave action and all the lei maker had to do was to punch out the grain of sand that may have lodged in the hole. More than two hundred shells were needed for one strand, thirty-six inches long, and several strands were required for the one lei.

Today, the pūpū Ni'ihau and lei pūpū o Ni'ihau are the official emblems of their native island. They have gained renewed popularity, and are strung in different patterns and sold in jewelry stores for much money.

The Hawaiians of old also strung up cone shells after drilling a hole in the base of each shell. The most commonly used cone shell was *Conus sponsalis.* Other cones used less often were *C. chaldaeus, C. miliaris, C. rattus, C. ebraeus,* and *C. catus.* The beach worn disks from the bases of cone shells were also used in a lei. The disks were strung through a hole in the center of each disk. The holes were naturally formed by wave and sand action or were drilled or punched out. Today, almost every youth and many older people in Hawai'i own a lei of cone shell disks which they call "puka shell necklace."

Pūpū mamāiki *(Strombus maculatus)* and *Polinices tumidus* are marine shells that were sometimes used by the lei maker.

White, green-brown, striped and solid colored pūpū kuahiwi, land shells, were gathered from the forests, holes were punched through the lip of each shell and strung on fine olonā cord to make the lei pūpū kuahiwi.

LEI HUA
(Seed Leis)

Seeds and nuts of various native plants strung on olonā cord made up a fourth type of permanent lei called lei hua. The most popular of this type was the lei kukui. The mature, blond, dark brown or black, shallow furrowed nuts of the candlenut *(Aleurites moluccana)* tree were painstakingly sanded down, polished, holes cut or punctured in the ends, nut meat removed and strung on a cord. The surface of the nut was treated and textured in a number of different ways. (see illustration, plate 4, d, page 12). The nut could retain its original shallow furrowed surface and shape. It could be sanded to a smooth surface then grooved lengthwise. It could be sanded with smooth panels running lengthwise following the curvature of the nut. It could be faceted like cut glass beads of diamonds. It could have elliptical grooves on the narrow side of the nut. Possibly it could have asterisk-like grooves on the top or bottom tips of the nut, radiating from the holes at either end.

The nuts were strung together which were all like treated, textured nuts on a single strand or mixed two or more different textured nuts repeated to make up a strand.

Lei pūpū o Nī'ihau

Lei pūpū o Nī'ihau

Lei kukui, smooth finis

Lei kupe'e

Lei Mānele

Lei kukui (grooved finish), Lei mānele and Lei wiliwili

The mature, dry nuts were gathered after falling from the trees. If the hulls remained intact, they were removed. Sometimes mature, green nuts were selected for their blond color, but it was the black nuts that were preferred.

The nuts were usually selected and segregated by like sizes, shapes, furrows and color. Removing the outer gray-white film was a painstaking procedure, considering the fact that the tools used were very primitive. Even with modern day tools and abrasives, this process is tedious. This step had to be completed if a smooth highly polished surface was desired. The nuts were grooved, faceted, or panelled with files made from sea urchin spines and sanded smooth with the tough skin of the kala (fish) or the shark, then finished with pumice. Holes were made by first cutting away, probably by grinding, the pointed end of the nut. The hole on the rounded end was then punctured out with a sharp tool from the inside out. The nut meat was broken into small pieces with a sharp tool and removed through the holes, or the nut was buried in the ground or left in a protected area. The nut meats would then decay or be eaten away by insects. The nuts were unearthed, wiped clean, then polished with a piece of kapa (bark cloth) soaked in kukui nut oil. The lei kukui was completed with the stringing of several nuts, enough to slip over the head and onto the shoulders, or enough nuts to make a choker type necklace which was tied around the neck, or to be worn breast length, waist length or one long strand worked in a double loop around the neck.

Other less notable seed and nut leis were made with other native materials, among them being the mānele or a'e *(Sapindus saponaria)*, soapberry; āulu, kaulu, lonomea *(Sapindus oahuensis)*; and wiliwili *(Erythrina sandwicensis)*.

Among the temporary leis of ancient Hawai'i were those that were reminiscent of other parts of Polynesia and those that were fashioned of materials that were endemic to Hawai'i. These were leis of flowers, leaves, and fruits. Most of the natural fresh materials were selected because they were beautifully scented. Other materials were selected for color and still others were selected for mobility. Some were selected for healing powers. The lasting quality of the material was least important.

Those that were reminiscent of other parts of Polynesia were maile *(Alyxia olivaeformis)*, hala *(Pandanus odoratissimus)*, hinahina *(Heliotropium anomalum* var. *argenteum)*, and ferns.

HALA, PANDANUS ODORATISSIMUS

The fruit of the hala was a popular lei material throughout Polynesia and other Pacific Islands. The hala tree could be found growing in groves at elevations from sea level to about 2,000 feet. The trees grow to heights of about twenty feet or more, and have many widespreading branches containing large heads of long, oftimes spinney, firm leaves and straight, cylindrical aerial roots. The mature, firm fruit provided the material used in leis. The drupes were separated and strung crosswise through the fleshy, fibrous end or each drupe was cut through that end (pua hala) with a shell or bamboo cutting edge. The length of the pua hala varied. This variation depended upon how much of the fleshy, fibrous end could be cut free from the nut end (iwi hala). The iwi hala was cast aside. Coconut midrib needles were used to string the pua hala longitudinally on lengths of bast from the hau, banana, or the roots of the pandanus tree. The pua hala was usually combined with bits of laua'e fern *(Microsorium scolopendria)*. The pungent fragrance of the pua hala and the gentle maile like fragrance of the laua'e produced a rich essence.

With the introduction of iron and the steel blade by western voyagers, the lei hala took on a new look. The pua hala was cut with a fluted or irregular scalloped (niho-niho) edge. The scallops were pointed as often as they were rounded.

The hala was a symbol and token of love. The pungent odor of the male blossom (hinano) and the ripe fruit (hala) was said to arouse love-making among the natives of old. "When the hala is ripe, necks are red (with garlands)" is an old saying which meant the time was right for love-making.

Since hala also means "fault, transgression, error; to pass," the stigma of the word meaning was attached to the lei. It was considered unlucky to wear the lei hala. This consideration probably resulted from a legend which tells of a kahuna lapa'au, medical priest, who asked Hi'iaka to help save his sick patient. Hi'iaka, who was wearing a lei hala, replied that she could not help him. It was too late, the patient had passed away.

The hala was favored by the Hi'iaka sisters. When the fishermen saw the pūhala fruiting and dropping its seeds to the ground, they knew that Hi'iaka-mākole-wāwahi-waka (Hi'iaka-the-red-eyed-who-smashes-canoes) was about, and if they took to the sea at this time, the waters would be rough and their canoes would be battered and smashed. It is Hi'iaka-i-ka-poli-o-pele (Hi'iaka-in-the-bosom-of-Pele) who in search for Pele's dream lover, Lohi'au, prince of Kaua'i, happened upon a maimed woman dancing and singing on the rocky beach of Kahakuloa, Maui. The pathetic sight of the dancing crippled woman touched the soul of Hi'iaka causing her to pluck on impulse from the hala lei about her neck a segment which she cast to the woman. The maimed woman gathered up the hala segment, breathed in the aroma. Grateful for being recognized by Hi'iaka, she sang:

"Ke lei mai la o Ka-ula i ke kai, e!
O ka malamalama o Ni'ihau, ua malie.
A malie, pa ka Inu-wai.
Ke inu mai le na hala o Naue i ke kai.
No Naue ka hala, no Puna ka wahine,
No ka lua i Kilauea.

Wearing the Lei niho palaoa (top photo); Lei niho palaoa (left); Lei niho palaoa (bottom right).

Lei hulu manu—Lei paukū or Lei pāwehe (top left); Lei hulu manu—(top) Lei mamo and (bottom) Lei pāni'o (top right); Lei hulu manu for the Neck (bottom left); Lei hulu manu for the Head (bottom right).

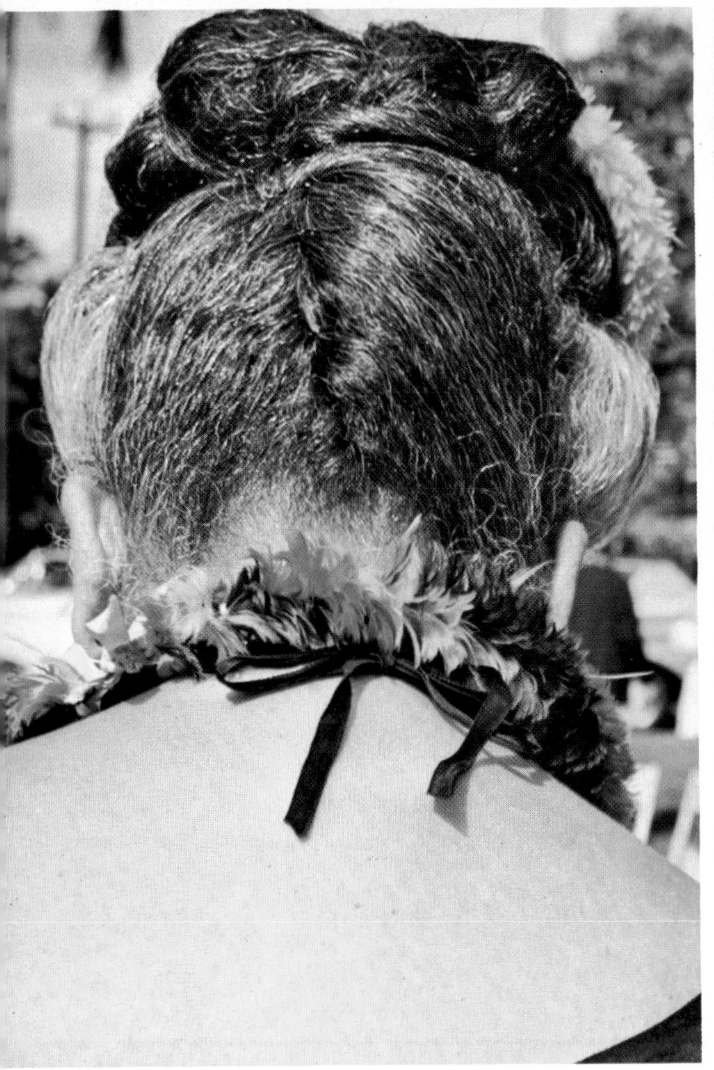

Ka'ula wreathes her brow with the ocean;
Ni'ihau shines forth in the calm.
After the calm blows the Inuwai.
And the palms of Naue drink of the salt.
From Naue the palm, from Puna the maid,
Aye from the pit of Kilauea."[1]

This mele (song) was to be used later by the dancers in their dressing ceremony. The song was sung as they knotted the leis about their heads and shoulders.

N.B. Emerson in Pele and Hi'iaka, a Myth from Hawaii, records this chant with the following footnote.

"He ahui hala ko Kapo-ula-kinau'u,
Ko ka pili kaumaha;
I ka pili a hala, la, ha-la!
Hala olua, aohe, makamaka o ka hale
I kou hale, e-e!"

The clustered hala is Kapo's shield,
An omen pretending disaster.
The traveler came in your absence;
Both of you gone, no one at home—
No lodge for the traveler within,
No hospitality within!

"HALA. The fruit of the hala was so often worn in the form of a wreath by Kapo that it came to be looked upon almost as her emblem. To ordinary mortals, this practice savored of bad luck. If a fisherman travelling on his way to the ocean were to meet a person wearing a lei of this description, he would feel compelled to turn back and give up his excursion for that day. In this instance, Kapo was on her way to visit a sick man—a bad omen for him."

Yet, there is the lucky side of the lei hala, again, derived from the word meaning. The lei hala worn during the makahiki (harvest, peace) festival meant that the faults, transgressions, troubles of the year gone by had passed away. The new year was approached without trouble and errors, with only good luck.

[1]Page 56 and Page 212, Unwritten Literature of Hawai'i, by Nathaniel B. Emerson.

To this day, Hawaiians still attach these meanings to the lei hala, and as the times and life modes changed, new lucky and unlucky occasions were added. "Never give a lei hala to a person who is campaigning for public office for it will surely mean his defeat." "Give a lei hala to wipe away misfortune and to herald good luck." "Give a lei hala to mark the passing, the completion of a venture and the beginning of a new one."

Legend tells of a king of the island of Hawai'i, Lono-i-ka-makahiki who relied in part on two leis to help him conquer the island of O'ahu. No battle clubs and spears ensued, instead a battle of wits and wagers.

Lono-i-ka-makahiki's first wager with Kākuhihewa, king of O'ahu, was for the section of land from Ka'ena Point to Ka'ō'io as against an ahi, yellow fin tuna, caught off O'ahu's shores. Kākuhihewa, after consulting with his advisors, felt sure that he would win the wager, since every one knew that ahi were caught only off the shores of Ni'ihau and Kaua'i. He agreed to the bet.

Lono-i-ka-makahiki pulled on his line and allowed the fish to pass alongside Kākuhihewa's canoe. Most certainly it was an ahi. The king of O'ahu lost his wager.

Lono-i-ka-makahiki brought the fish alongside his canoe quickly, so that the occupants of the other canoe could not see, and he draped a lei of lehua and one of hala around the fish's head. The leis were prepared beforehand expressly for this purpose. Now, he was ready for the second wager.

Lono-i-ka-makahiki called out to Kākuhihewa telling him that the fish was a yellow-gilled ahi of Umulau, Hawai'i for it was wearing wreaths of lehua and hala. The king of O'ahu felt certain that the king of Hawai'i was deceiving him. His companions agreed. So he made another wager. This time the section of land from Ka'ō'io Point to Mōkapu Point. Needless to say, the king of Hawai'i won the bet.

The goading of the king of Hawai'i and the

betting by the king of O'ahu continued until all of O'ahu was won by Lono-i-ka-makahiki.

From another Hawaiian myth, Kakele, a quiet handsome woman and wife of Kaulu, a spirit being, planted the hala groves of Ko'olau, O'ahu, remnant descendants of which still grow today. She wore leis of sweet smelling pandanus.

On the eve of each new year, Mama and Daddy would join their friends for a round of well wishing, and that was truly what it was. From house to house they would go, singing as they made the rounds the favorite songs of Hawai'i, "Nani wale ku'u home 'Āina-Hau i ka 'iu . . . Pua wale mai nō ke aloha . . . Ku'u pua ku'u lei, ku'u milimili e, . . . Mau loa no ko'u mahalo nui . . . Pūpū (a'o 'Ewa), i ka nu'a (nā kānaka) . . ." The songs would spill out one after the other from the very depths of each one of them. Uncle Afat's rich baritone and Auntie Aholo's sweet soprano voices kept all the others together.

In later years, we children joined them in the tradition of eve of the New Year. We ushered in the new year by serenading with friends and family and by celebrating at the stroke of twelve with a grand lū'au (feast) at our house or someone elses. Aineiki and Hester seemed to attract the young cowboys from the ranch. They became a part of our celebration and soon the serenaders in the evening took to horseback with hala and maile leis on hats, heads and about the necks of both riders and horses.

Hala Tree (top left); Pūhala with laua'e fern (bottom right).

Stringing the hala segments

ala (top left); Lei hala (uncut drupes)—(bottom).

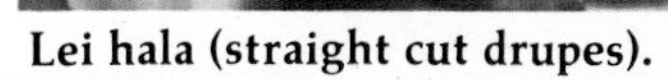

Lei hala (straight cut drupes).

LEHUA, 'ŌHI'A LEHUA, METROSIDEROS SPP.

One of the most common and extremely variable groups of native plants, the 'ohi'a lehua ranges in heights of a few inches in the boglands, to scrubby shrubs in the dry forest, to magnificent trees of well over one hundred feet in the wet forests. The small leaves vary in shape from round to narrow, pointed to blunt, with smooth or wooly undersides, and red to yellow veins and stems. The young, new leaf buds vary in color from silver-white to pink and red. Flowers are clustered and appear to be all stamen, ranging in size from one-half inch to one inch long. Red flowers are more common than salmon, pink, yellow, or white. There are many varieties of lehua: lehua 'āhihi, a weeping variety having markedly red stems; lehua-'āpane, a variety having deep red flowers; lehua-ha'akea, lehua kea, lehua-puakea, a variety having white flowers; lehua-ku-ma-kua, a variety with heart-shaped leaves connected directly to the main stem; lehua-lau-li'i, a variety with very small leaves; lehua-maka-noe, lehua-ne'ene'e, the variety that grows in the bogs; lehua-mamo, a variety with yellow flowers; lehua-papa, a variety from the high forest of the Ko'olau Mountains of O'ahu with round, leathery, grooved leaves.

The pua lehua, flowers; the lau lehua, mature leaves; the liko lehua, the young leaves and buds; and the hua lehua, or seed capsules, were all used in lei making. The pua lehua and the liko lehua were preferred for their brilliant color, nectar-like scent and symbolism of strength.

The lei lehua was made by tying clusters of leaves and flowers by their stems to a central cord, or by securing clusters of leaves and flowers by their stems into a plait of fern or other natural materials, or by sewing them down to a central cord. Rarely, were the blossoms pierced and strung on a cord.

The groves of lehua at Puna, Hawai'i were prized possessions of Hi'iaka-i-ka-poli-o-Pele given to her by her sister, Pele, goddess of the volcanoes to whom the lehua was sacred. The lei lehua was tossed into the crater at Kilauea as an offering to Pele.

In the Legend of Pele and Hi'iaka, Pele sends Hi'iaka to search for her dream lover, Lohi'au. Hi'iaka's search takes longer than anticipated. Hi'iaka resists the advances of Lohi'au, but Pele suspects betrayal. In a fit of jealousy and rage, Pele destroys the two things that Hi'iaka loves most—Hōpoe, the hula teacher and dearest friend, and the Puna groves of lehua. Hi'iaka declares the pact between them broken and swears revenge. She sits with Lohi'au at the brink of the caldera in full view of Pele and her court. She has woven three leis of scarlet lehua blossoms. With a smile on her face, she drapes two of the leis around the neck of Lohi'au. The third lei, she keeps for herself. She urges Lohi'au to come closer as she ties the knot and secures the leis about his neck. She sings. Emotion fills her song.

"O Hi'iaka ka wahine,
Ke apo la i ka pua;
Ke kui la, ke uo la i ka manai.
Eha ka lei, ka apana lehua lei
A ka wahine la, ku'u wahine,
Ku'u wahine o ka ehu makani o
lalo.
Lulumi aku la kai o Hilo-one;
No Hilo ke aloha—aloha wale
ka lei, e!

'Twas a maid Hi'iaka plucked the
bloom;
This wreath her very hands did
weave;
Her needle 'twas that pierced
each flower;
Her's the fillet that bound them
in one.
Four strands of lehua make the
lei—
The wreath bound on by this maid—

Maid who once basked in the calme
down there:
Her heart harks back to Hilo-one
Wreath and heart are for Hilo-
one."[2]

The lehua, in ancient times, was a symbol of strength. This fragment from a mele inoa, a name song, composed in honor of Liloa and later passed down to 'Umi and on to Kalani-nui-a-mamao illustrates the symbolism of the lehua.

"A garland strung of red flowers thou,
The bank on which rests the island,
The bamboo buoys of the Kanaloa,
The Kanaloa of Kane,
Kane of the fruitful growing month,
Month that of Kaelo."[3]

"A garland strung of red flowers thou" poetically describes Liloa as a beloved one of great strength. The red flowers, the lehua.

The poets and storytellers of old, when expounding the wonders of the island of Hawai'i, the domain of Pele and the dwelling place of Hi'iaka-i-ka-poli-o-Pele, would never fail to attach to their descriptions the beauty of the red lehua blossoms. Since this early attachment of the red lehua to Hawai'i, and because of its prevalence on this island from the mountain to the sea, the red lehua has become the official flower of the island of Hawai'i.

Ancient lore forbids the plucking of the red lehua blossom and the wearing of the lei lehua when going to Kilauea, for it will surely rain. After reaching the crater, leis of lehua can be and were made, then thrown into the pit as offerings to Pele. Ancient lore did not forbid the gathering of blossoms and the wearing of the lehua lei when returning from Kilauea. It was encouraged, for it was proof that one had visited with Pele at the crater.

In the kupua, supernatural being, story of Kalele-a-lua-ka, Ka-o-pele-moemoe falls into a trance and sleeps for six months When he awakens, his parents find him in a tree braiding scarlet lehua flowers into a lei.

Ka-o-pele-moemoe has a son, Kalele-a-lua-ka, who grows up to be a mischievous boy. Because of his supernatural powers, he can jump up and down precipices. Kalele-a-lua-ka marries the daughter of Kākuhihewa, chief of O'ahu. Using his special powers and disguising himself with leis of different localities, he carries Kākuhihewa's lame marshall to oversee battles at Wai'anae, Waialua, Kahuku, and Pu'uowaina. At Wai'anae, he arrays himself with leis of maile lauli'i which is peculiar to that region. At Waialua, he bedecks himself with leis of hinahina from Keālia and 'uki from the lagoon of 'Uko'a. At Kahuku, he wears hala leis about his neck and cane tassels on his head.

These disguises help him to win the battles in these districts, bringing them under the control of his chief, Kākuhihewa. His final battle was at Pu'uowaina where single handed he defeats the forces of Kuali'i.

Hi'iaka on her first trip to Hawai'i with her sister, Pele, and brother, Kāne-'āpua left a lei lehua at a tiny island west of Ni'ihau when she discovered that her brother had decided to stay on there. Since then the island has been called Lehua Island.

MAILE, ALYXIA OLIVAEFORMIS

Maile is probably the oldest and the most popular temporary material used in leis by the early Hawaiians. This straggling, vinelike shrub, grows in the forests of lower and middle elevations. The shiny, leathery leaves ranging in size from about one-half inch to sometimes four inches and the bark of the plant was used to make the lei. The bark and leaves are stripped free from the young shoots of the plant. The process usually takes place in the mountains where the plant grows. The young shoots are held close to their base ends with the thumb and index fin-

[2] N.B. Emerson, Myth of Pele and Hi'iaka.
[3] Page 140, David Malo-Hawaiian Antiquities. Translation and notes by N.B. Emerson.

'Ohi'a lehua Trees

Red lehua blossoms (top right); Lei with yellow lehua blossoms, māmane blossoms and uluhe and palapalai ferns (center).

Lei lehua with palapalai fern

Yellow lehua blossoms (top left); White liko lehua (center); Red liko lehua (top right).

Dancers with Lei liko lehua

ger. A twist around the circumference of the shoot and a sliding motion from the base of the shoot toward the tip with thumb and index finger tightly grasping the shoot, frees the bark and leaves from the woody core.

Several such lengths are removed from the plants in the forest. They are gathered together, wrapped in tī leaf sacks, and taken home where they are tied together in lengths long enough to drape around the neck or wind around the head. Usually three or more knotted lengths are twisted or braided together to make a single lei.

Sometimes the young shoots are cut from the shrub and the removal of the bark and leaves is done by gently pounding the shoots with a stone or wooden mallet or by rolling over the shoots with a wooden rolling pin thus smashing the stem. The pounding or rolling loosens the bark from the woody core and the stripping is made easier.

The maile from each of the islands seemed to have minute differences, which in some cases, are not easily distinguished by the inexperienced lei wearer. The maile from Hawai'i is large leafed, from Kaua'i it is round and small leafed, from O'ahu is middle sized leaf. There is maile lau nui, large leaves; maile lau li'i, small leaves; maile lau li'ili'i, very small leaves. There is brittle maile, maile ha'i wale, luxuriant maile, greedy maile and sweet leaved maile, maile kaluhea..

The lei maile was the lei of all the people, the upper classes as well as the lower classes. Maile was associated with worship of the gods, especially the gods of the hula. It was sacred to Laka and was offered at her altar with other plants of the native forest. It was worn by the dancers who paid homage to her.

"O Laka ke akua pule ikaika,
Ua ku ka maile a Laka a imua,
Ua lu ka hua o ka maile . . . .

The prayer to the goddess Laka has power,
The maile of Laka stands foremost,
The goddess inspires her pupil as the maile scatters its fragrance . . . ."[4]

The lei maile was a peace offering on the field of battle.

In the Romance of Lā'ie-i-ka-wai, a story of a high kapu chiefess and her suitor, 'Aiwohikupua, a demigod goes to woo Lā'ie-i-ka-wai but is rebuffed despite the presence of his four maile sisters. 'Aiwohikupua is enraged by the insult and becomes angry with his sisters for not being able to help him in his courtship. He abandons them in the forest, where they are still to be found today. A fifth sister, Ka-hala-o-māpuana, refuses to leave her sisters. She, being the cleverest of the five girls, manages to attract the attention of Lā'ie-i-ka-wai who adopts them and makes them the guardians of Paliuli, the earthly dwelling place of Lā'ie-i-ka-wai in the uplands of Puna. With Kiha-nui-lulu-moku, the lizard, the five sisters protect Lā'ie-i-ka-wai from unfavorable suitors.

Hence the association of sweet scented plant materials with courtship and love-making. It could be said that the maile and the hala were used in ancient times much as French perfume is used today.

The four maile sisters were Maile-ha'i-wale, brittle maile, Maile-pākaha, many branched maile, Maile-kaluhea, large leafed, fragrant maile, and Maile-lau-li'i, small leafed maile.

Maile is associated with the worship of the gods. It is said that if one smells maile where it cannot be seen or where it evidently does not grow, here then is the site of an ancient temple.

I do not remember my first maile lei. It seems that it was always there. My mother would call someone and there it was, ready for the birthday, the graduation, the wedding, the anniversary, the hellos and the good-byes and all the other special

[4] N.B. Emerson, Unwritten Literature of Hawai'i.

occasions that warranted a maile lei. Ready to entwine with hala or pīkake or kīkānia or pakalana or freesias. The maile with its gentle fragrance enhanced the fragrance of the other leis. When we wanted it or needed it, it was there.

For years, I acted as if I knew all about the maile lei and the where, the why and the how you gathered maile. I had some recollection of mama stripping it by gently pounding the young branches with a smooth, round stone, but it wasn't until some thirty years after my birth that I actually found some growing in the mountains high above Waikolu on Moloka'i. My childhood friend and then Ranch Ranger, Harry Joao, was talked into taking me with him on his regular rounds of checking the water tanks and gauges along the mountain ridge.

I was in the midst of discovering the Hawai'i of my heritage and any opportunity to discover more increased my curiosity and my enthusiasm. The excitement and awe that accompanied the discovery of even a simple fact was many times overwhelming. And this trip with Harry was overwhelming.

Before the sun had come up, we were already on our way. We stopped at Mahana, then we cut back across the Ho'olehua plain, through Kualapupu'u and up to Kala'e. As we bounced along, Harry told some folk tales, not pre-Cook kind, but present Harry Joao kind. We had to go through several locked gates. We drove past Meyer Lake and I was not impressed. I had expected something bigger. I had heard of this lake many times over while I was growing up on this island, but this was the first time that I had come this way and there it was. It looked like a large mud puddle to me and Harry read the disappointment on my face. He reminded me that it was summer. In the winter time, the heavy rains would fill the bottom land and the lake would increase in size, sometimes tenfold. Okay, Harry, I smiled to myself.

You could tell that this man loved his land. His love for it poured out as he pointed out the yellow, the orange and the brilliant red pua lehua. His eyes challenged me, have you ever seen such beauty? And I answered out loud, "Harry it is fantastic!" In some places 'ōhelo lined the jeep roadside and the bushes were covered with pink and orange and red berries. We drove along the ridge for a little while overlooking Kalaupapa, then we were lost in the dense forest. The forest was like Harry and me in lineage, it had some Hawaiian mixed in with the haole. There were stands of pine and cypress of the North American variety with white and yellow gingers from Asia growing under them. I caught my breath at the sight of flowering clumps of New Zealand flax, tall maroon spires with deep red flowers.

We stopped and Harry ordered me out. "We're going to pick maile," he said and continued with, "some Democrats are having a rally this weekend." About ten feet off the jeep road, he started to yank on the new growth of vinelike plants and then, I smelled it. "Show me how," I called as I stumbled behind him. He did. We went in opposite directions while stripping the bark and leaves free from their woody stems.

An hour or so had gone by when Harry returned, his shirt tucked in at the waist and bulging under the arms with maile lau li'i. He smelled better than any cologne could make him smell. He emptied his shirt full of maile into the jeep. The scent lingered on his body as we bumped along the road.

I asked Harry about some very small leafed maile. I remembered that, many years ago, my mother wrapped a fragrant, yellow freesia lei with a single strand of maile with very tiny leaves. Harry smiled and nodding his head he said, "I show you. That maile lau li'ili'i grows down at a lower elevation and it's drier there. In April and May, after the heavy rains that maile can be stripped easy, but now it's too dry and the maile is too brittle. I show you anyway."

Maile vine (top left); Stripping maile (top right); Lei Maile (center); Lei with maile and ferns (bottom).

Knotting lengths of maile (top left); Dancers with maile leis (bottom).

We stopped to peer down into steep Waikolu Valley and Harry showed me the land shells that clung to naupaka-kuahiwi leaves. We continued. Harry wanted me to see everything. We stopped at the old C.C.C. Camp and I gathered a handful of ginger blossoms. We looked into a big rectangular pit, the size of a cargo hold on the old sailing ships that took part in the China trade and Harry said, "they cut down the sandalwood forest and placed the timber in this hole, then they knew that they were ready to send for a ship to carry it away some place."

We continued back up the rut filled road, then down toward the sea on the lee side we came, through fields of stunted 'a'ali'i and koko'olau. Harry stopped and I gathered up an armful of 'a'a-li'i while he unlocked a gate. The road became steep and rocky. Harry stopped again. This time at a dry stream bed. "Come on," he said, "I show you the maile lau li'ili'i." There it was.

Still many years later I made a mental comparison of this maile, the maile I had gathered at Kaupō Gap in the crater of Haleakalā on Mau'i, the maile I had often gathered in the Wai'anae range on O'ahu and the maile I was stripping in a kīpuka in the Waiakea Forest on Hawai'i. Which of these did I prefer? I never could decide. Each was beautiful, but the adventures, and the people, that were associated with my maile experiences were far more beautiful.

'ILIMA, SIDA SPP.

A number of different kinds of 'ilima plants are found growing along the rocky and sandy beach coast to altitudes of more than 2,000 feet. Flowers have five petals, measure about one inch across and are the thickness of tissue paper. They range in color from yellow to deep gold to rusty orange and are rarely greenish. Plants range in heights from low prostrate creepers to about four feet or more.

Flowers from all types may have been used for lei making; however, preference was given to the deep gold 'ilima lei and the rusty 'ilima-koli-kukui. These were probably the only plants that were cultivated by the early Hawaiians especially for lei flowers. All other lei materials were gathered from plants growing in a wild state in the fields, deep valleys, along the seashore and in the forests.

The flowers are sometimes gathered as tight buds in the evening. Most lei makers, however, prefer to gather the flowers in the early morning before the sun comes up. Lei makers found it more efficient to remove the calyx from partially rather than fully opened blossoms since it is easier to hold on to them than it is to hold the paper-thin fully bloomed blossom. Also, there is less chance of bruising the petals when the flowers are still unopened. The flowers reach full bloom as the morning wears on. The blossoms last through the day, then they wither and die. Thus, the answer to this old Hawaiian riddle:

> *"In the evening, gathered;*
> *In the morning, pierced;*
> *In the forenoon, hung in the air."*

is the lei 'ilima.

Many hundreds of blossoms are needed to make a single strand of breast length. The calyx of each blossom is removed except for the first and last blossom. These and a bud were used as stoppers to keep the blossoms from slipping from the bast on which they were strung. The blossoms were pierced through the center, starting at the base end.

Because the gathering of the flowers and the making of this lei was a painstaking labor of love, and because the blossoms were of fragile and very temporary beauty and rich brilliant color, the lei 'ilima became a highly prized possession of the royal and educated classes of Hawaiian society. It was not, however, restricted for their use only. It, like the maile lei, was for all people. It was sacred to Laka, was worn by her dancers and offered at her altar in the hālau hula.

The haku mele, poets of ancient times, called, according to Pukui and Elbert, the 'ilima, pua 'apiki and the lei 'ilima, lei 'apiki, "because it was believed to attract mischievous spirits: some did not wear this lei, but others considered it lucky."[5] The haku mele then as well as those of today, attached the pua 'ilima and the lei 'ilima to the island of O'ahu. A poetic description of the island would invariably include the wondrous beauty of the lei 'ilima. Today, the 'ilima is the official flower of O'ahu.

I was born in the manager's house at Waikele on O'ahu. The manager was my father and he managed the Waipahu branch of the Mutual Telephone Company. I was the fifth child born to Etelka and John Adams. Before me were Aineiki, Hester, John, and Jo (Josephine). Irma followed me. She was born in a hospital. Then came Dick, Jim and Scott who were born in the house where I was born. My brother Michael came years later on Moloka'i. We lived at Waikele for six years and we played with Maka, short for Maka-'ele'ele, Kilipohe, and Kalele, short for Ka-lele-o-na-pā. John played with Maka and Kalele, the boys, while Jo, Irma and I played with their sister, Kilipohe. Their mother must have been a lei lady, for she was always stringing 'ilima leis. Her front yard was filled with 'ilima bushes that were taller than I. I don't think that I have ever seen bushes as tall as those since, but I was only five then and everything that children remember are always bigger than big.

On occasion, we had fun helping to pick the not fully opened rust and orange flowers in the early, early morning, but Maka, Kilipohe and Kalele found it a chore since they had to do it every day. Sometimes, Maka and Kalele would run away to play with John. And, sometimes, they would run right back, for John teased them with cruel childish ditties, "Maka-'ele'ele, young tar ball." Maka was a young, dark lad with laughing black eyes. "Kalele-o-na-pā hanging on the car." John had seen Kalele hanging on to the inside of an automobile door as it swung open while the car was in motion. He thought it was funny. So whenever they fought, as children did, he teased.

When we left Waikele to move to Moloka'i, and a new superintendent's post for my father, someone or ones gifted us with 'ilima leis. We like to think that they were Maka-'ele'ele, Kilipohe and Ka-lele-o-na-pā.

KĪ, LĀ'Ī, TĪ, CORDYLINE TERMINALIS

A shrubby plant found throughout tropical Asia and tropical areas of the Pacific basin. It grows in the lush valleys and mountainsides to heights of about twelve feet. It has narrow oblong leaves of about one and one-half feet to two feet long growing in spiraled clusters from the tips of its branches. The leaves, lau kī, lau'ī, la'ī, had a variety of uses, from packages for cooking and carrying, to plates, to raincoats and sandals.

The Hawaiians believed that the tī plant had powers to heal and to ward off evil spirits. The tī was the sacred symbol of the gods. The leaves were used in the rituals of cleansing and rendering free of evil spirits by the kahuna-pule heiau, temple priest, and in the rituals of healing by the kahuna-lapa'au, the medical priest. The people of old planted hedges of tī plants around their houses to keep out the evil spirits. The kahuna-pule heiau and the kahuna-lapa'au wore leis of lā'ī or carried a stalk of leaves or a single leaf on ceremonious occasions as the sacred symbol of the gods and almost as an emblem of their profession or their rank.

The lei lā'ī for the neck was made with two leaves. The midrib was removed from the undersides of the leaves. The leaves were stripped or not. The stem ends were knotted together to form one long length. The knotted stem ends were placed at the nape of the neck while the leaf ends were draped down the front of the chest. The lei lā'ī was worn open-ended in horseshoe fashion.

[5] Page 26, 1957 Hawaiian-English Dictionary.

'Ilima kūkahakai (top left); 'Ilima flower (top right); Stringing 'ilima blossoms (center left); Lei kou (center right); Lei 'ilima (bottom left); Kou blossoms (bottom right).

Wearing strands of 'ilima

Tī plants
(Above);
Kahuna wearing
Lei lā'ī (below).

Lei lāʻī, an offering at the kuʻula

The lei lā'ī for the head was made from a single leaf, midrib removed. The stem end was tied to the tip end of the leaf securely around the head. A head lei of this kind was also used for relief from headaches and fever. The coolness of the leaf seemed to have therapeutic powers.

In the housing compounds of each family was a small house called the hale pe'a which was used by the women during their menstral periods. Here the women remained in isolation. During this period of confinement, they wore leis of lā'ī to protect them from uncleanliness. If it were necessary for them to travel during these periods, and especially if they had to cross Pele's domain, the lei lā'ī went with them, for the tī would summon the protection of the volcano goddess.

The green tī leaves were necessary in the decorating of the altar of Laka in the halau hula. No ceremonial serving of 'awa was complete without a properly woven base of tī leaves to support the 'awa bowl.

The tī leaves were used as the central cord to which plant materials were sewn, tied, or plaited.

KOU, CORDIA SUBCORDATA

The evergreen kou tree was probably brought to Hawai'i by the early Polynesian immigrants. Trees grow to heights of about thirty feet. They were popular shade trees for villages along the leeward coasts of the island chain. The pumpkin orange, scentless blossoms were used to make a lei that was preferred for its brilliant color. The flowers which measure one to two inches in diameter at the mouth, were usually gathered in the evening after they had fallen from the trees. The flowers which were strung lengthwise through the center resemble a modern day crepe paper or an enlarged 'ilima lei.

There is a legend which tells of a young chiefess of Ewa O'ahu who saw an old lady stringing a lei of Kou blossoms. The chiefess who was on her way to bathe in the sea, stopped to ask the old lady for the lei. The old woman angrily told her to get her own flowers and make her own lei. The chiefess bathed and returned to ask for the lei once more. The answer was again an angry one. Once more the chiefess bathed and returned to ask for the lei. Little did the chiefess know that the old woman was a sorcerer and could cause sharks to appear. The chiefess sat close to the water's edge with her long black hair hanging in the water. The sharks appeared, asked the old woman what they should do with the teasing girl. The old woman told them to do as they wished. The sharks ate the girl and scattered her blood over the bank where the soil remains red to this day. It is said that no one in Ewa wears the lei kou.

My sisters and I associate the lei kou with happy times—summer and the movies at the open-air theater at Kaunakakai.

It wasn't often that Dad would allow us to go to the movies. There were so many of us and each of us under twelve years old had to pay ten cents to get into the Kukui Theater. In 1936 ten cents was still a lot of money. But when Dad said, "yes," Irma, Jo and I would immediately become involved in what seemed to be a strange ritual. We would scurry about collecting flowers to string into leis.

In the summer time, the kou blossoms were our favorite. The trees that grew in our yard, one at the front door of our house and the other right next to the building that housed my father's office and the telephone company's switchboard, always had a lot of flowers. Each late afternoon, the flowers would break free from their calyxes and fall to the ground. On special occasions, such as going to the movies, we would gather enough flowers for leis for each of us. Sometimes some of the blossoms had not fallen to the ground and Jo, the oldest of the three of us, would order Irma and me up the tree to shake them loose. Hannah Meyer, the clerk-stenographer in Dad's office would peer out of the window and shout her usual words of cau-

tion. We pretended not to hear her, as all children our age usually did, and went about the business of shaking free the pumpkin-orange blossoms. Jo would gather the flowers as we shook and would add them to the mound on the grass.

Then, with coconut nī'au needles and crochet thread from mama's bag, we would string our leis, knowing that there were other kids our age and grownups too who were observing the same ritual in preparation for the movies at Kukui Theater. The homesteaders at Ho'olehua were gathering and stringing 'ākulikuli and carnations. The "titas" from Mana'e were cutting hala keys and plucking pakalana from the vines. The boys from the C.C.C. Camp at Ma'alehua were stringing yellow and white 'awapuhi and wrapping them with strands of maile. Mrs. Maioho and Mrs. Hanakahi of Kalama'ula were selecting pīkake buds. Then to the movies, all of us.

I cannot remember the movies we saw—Tom Mix, Flash Gordon, Clark Gable, the Dead End Kids—but I can remember that the fragrance of the leis, made more pungent by the night air, attracted the lovers to each other and dispelled the discomfort of the awkward wooden benches and the dusty dirt floor. And the stars overhead smiled down on us.

KAUNA'OA, DODDER, CUSCUTA SANDWICHIANA

Native to Hawai'i, this unusual plant is found growing wild in fields, along the roadsides and above the high water mark on the leeward beaches. It begins its growth with roots in the ground then it attaches itself to other plants. It is a parasite thriving on its host plant. The entire light orange beach variety is used to make the lei kauna'oa. The stringy, slender stems are twisted or braided together to make a length long enough to circle the head or to hang over the shoulders. A binding thread is not necessary to hold the stems together. Because of its parasitic qualities, the lei would bind itself if allowed to stand a few hours before wearing it.

In the legends and meles of old, the island of Lāna'i was noted for its kauna'oa. As a result, the official lei of that island today is the lei kauna'oa.

Kauna'oa-pehu, a very coarse dodder is frequently used for leis in contemporary times since it is more common than kauna'oa.

HINAHINA, HINAHINA-KU-KAHAKAI, HELIOTROPIUM ANOMALUM VAR. ARGENTEUM.

Prostrate perennial herbs growing on the dry sandy beaches just above the high water mark. The leaves are silvery gray. Small clusters of fragrant white flowers with yellow centers are borne on stems from one to two inches long. The unusual color of the leaves and the fragrance of the flowers made the hinahina a choice material for leis. To make the lei hinihina, branch ends with leaf clusters that resemble rossettes and stems with flowers are attached to a central cord with a thread by wrapping the thread around the stems and the central cord. A second method also was used. That of plaiting the stems into the center cord.

Because the plants grew profusely on the dry, arid island of Kaho'olawe, they became synonymous with it. Today, the flowers are the official flowers of Kaho'olawe.

MOKIHANA, PELEA ANISATA

A scraggly native tree growing to heights of about twenty feet, found only in the forests of Kaua'i. The tree bears small greenish flowers and leathery cube-shaped seed capsules. The anise scented seed capsules are pierced through the center and strung on a cord to make the lei that has in chants and legends been associated with Kaua'i. The lei was prized for its beautiful scent and was often stored away with tapa garments, serving as a sachet. Strands of mokihana were often interlaced with strands of maile. The scent of the two materials complemented each other.

Leis touching bare, moist skin may sometimes cause a "burn."

Lei kauna'oa-lei (top right)

Kauna'oa-lei growing on 'ilima and pōhue (center left); Twisting kauna'oa-lei (center right); Wearing a Lei kauna'oa-lei (bottom); Lei hinahina (bottom left of opposite page).

Wearing the lei hinahina (top left); Hinahina blossoms and fleshy leaves (top right); Hinahina growing on sand dunes (bottom right).

"Maika'i wale nō Kaua'i
Hemolele wale i ka mālie.
Kuahiwi nani, Wai'ale'ale,
Lei ana i ka mokihana."

So very beautiful is Kaua'i
So perfect in the calm.
Pretty mountain, Wai'ale'ale,
Wears the mokihana lei."

Adapted from an old chant, probably for Ka-umu-ali'i, King of Kaua'i.

KUKUI, CANDLENUT, ALEURITES MOLUCCANA

Introduced by the early Polynesian settlers, the kukui soon became one of the most common trees in the Hawaiian forest. Groves of kukui trees can easily be distinguished by the powdery light green masses that dot the mountainsides and valleys of all the islands. The leaves are usually angular pointed or lobed. Small creamy white flowers grow in clusters. Seeds are tough shelled nuts contained in fleshy hulls.

The lei kukui was made by braiding the leaves by their stems and inserting clusters of flowers into the braid. Other methods of making the lei were used, but this one seemed to be the most appropriate for the material.

The mature blond, brown to black nuts were polished to a high shine and strung on cords to make the favorite permanent lei described in an earlier part of this book.

The lei kukui is representative of the island of Moloka'i.

At an early age, my brother John was a charming fellow. He could charm anyone into doing his bidding. So good was he, we were certain that he could charm a bumble bee into giving him honey. Thus, he was elected by a bunch of us who were all home for the summer from school in Honolulu to go down the street and ask Daisy if we could borrow her truck.

The truck was ours. Well, a truck of sorts was ours. It was a Ford sedan. The back end had been cut away and a wooden bed had been added. It had no horn, but that didn't bother us. We would yell and scream at the cows and pigs if they should bar our journey to Halawa.

We all jumped in. At first, the road was nice. It was smooth macadam until just before Kamalō. There the nice road ended and the ruts and bumps began. David, John's friend, strummed his ukulele and we sang, ". . . . me Moloka'i nui a Hina, 'āina i ka wehiwehi, e ho'i nō au e pili . . . ." until we began to descend from Pu'u-o-hōkū to the floor of Halawa Valley. The singing ceased, for now our voices had to substitute for the horn that wasn't there as we rounded the numerous blind hairpin turns. The winding road was bumpy with shear drops to the ocean on one side and straight up cliff walls on the other. Morning rain had fallen and the air smelled of wet earth and 'ākia blossoms.

We reached the valley floor, passed the country school house and old church, then parked our borrowed truck of sorts beyond the ironwood trees close to the spot where the stream emptied into the ocean. We were surrounded by spider lilies, pōhuehue and maunaloa vines. The ten of us, all teenagers, stumbled out of the truck, shook our legs free of knots and kinks, gathered together our lard cans, and began the hike to Moa'ula Falls. Our mission? Fill our lard cans with red, sweet 'ōhi'a'ai, mountain apples, and frolick in the chilling yet warming pool at the base of the falls.

We crossed the swinging bridge and zig-zagged our way over the dried, packed mud dikes through the taro lo'i to the beginning of the trail. The hike is warm and dry at first. Pānini and sisal stand as sentinals along the trail. The deeper we delve into the valley, the cooler and moister it gets. The sentinals change to hordes of 'ulu, kukui, mango and Surinam cherry. Laua'e and pala'ā line the trail while palapalai hide in the deep shade of the towering trees. Patches of yellow and white ginger reach out from the moist humus covered earth into the stream.

Mokihana seeds

Lei mokihana (top right); Wearing the Lei mokihana (bottom).

We line the lard cans with tī leaves and ferns and fill them with fruit. The extra fruit are wrapped in some pū'olo made of tī leaves. We swim in the chilling mountain pool and as we emerge from the water, the warmth that surges through our bodies cannot be described. We gather ferns and ginger blossoms, kukui leaves and flowers, and plait the leis that are typical of the deep valleys on all the Islands. We whack our heads with 'awapuhi, then scrub them with the sudsy slime that ooze from the bracts. We don our leis and dive back into the cold pool to swim once more.

At home again, Mama would gather us up and breathe in the clean fresh odor of 'awapuhi and fern, ginger and kukui, and remember the times that she and Dad went with us. We made this pilgrimage to Halawa each year that we lived on Moloka'i and two or three times later when we took our spouses and children to re-live a part of our young lives.

'A'ALI'I, DODONEA SPP.

Ranging in heights of one to thirty feet, this shrub to tree is found growing at elevations up to 8,000 feet. It is a common plant of the Hawaiian forest and wind-swept open country. Leaves are elongated, blunt or pointed, about one to four inches by .25 to one inch. Flowers are small, appear in clusters at branch tips or leaf axils. It is the two-to-four winged seed capsules ranging in color from yellow, pink, brown to very dark red that is used to make the lei 'a'ali'i. Sometimes clusters of the tiny flowers are used because they have a very subtle talcum powder fragrance.

The seed capsules were strung one by one or the clusters of fruits and flowers were braided or tied in a central cord of ferns, dried banana skin, tī leaves or other such materials. The finished lei was papery in texture and weight.

Kukui leaves and flowers (left); Kukui trees (right).

Wearing the Lei kukui in pageantry

'ŌLAPA, LAPALAPA, CHEIRODENDRON SPP.

Dominant trees of the Hawaiian wet forest of 4,000 to 6,000 feet elevations, the 'ōlapa and lapalapa are easily recognized by their constant quaking. Trees grow to 40 or 50 feet tall with opposite leaves each palmately divided into three to five leaflets which are oval to oblong in one species and heart-shape in another. Leaf petioles are flattened and very supple which accounts for the fluttering leaves that readily distinguishes these trees from others of the wet forest. Fruits are clustered, ranging in color from green to deep purple depending upon their maturity.

It is said that the group of hula called "'ōlapa" gets its name from these trees because the body movements of the dancers imitate the graceful movements of the 'ōlapa leaves. In the slightest breeze, the leaves of most species quiver. As wind speeds mount, the movement of the leaves become hysterical.

The musicians and dancers wore the lei fashioned from the 'ōlapa and lapalapa leaves which was prized for its movements and its attachment to the hula. The lei was made by knotting the stems of the leaves together.

In the Marquesas Islands, a similar lei was made with the leaves of the pimata *(Cheirodendron marquiesense)* where it also was valued for its movement.

PALAPALAI, PALAI, MICROLEPIA SETOSA

A native fern found growing on the edge of the mountain forests and in present day gardens. It is a lacey fern which grows to about three to four feet high. It was sacred to Laka and was used to decorate the altar in the hula halau *(dance hall)* along with several other native plant materials.

The lei palapalai was favored by the dancers. The fern was used as a single material in

Lei kukui with pūkiawe (left); Lei kukui (right).

Wearing the Lei kukui for fun

Wearing the Lei ʻaʻaliʻi (top); ʻAʻaliʻi, winged seed pods (bottom).

ʻŌlapa tree

(Top to bottom) Lei ʻaʻaliʻi, wili style; Lei ʻaʻaliʻi, kui pololei style; Lei ʻōlapa.

Wearing the Lei ʻōlapa

Making a Fern Lei (top left); Palapalai Ferns (top right).

Laua'e Ferns (bottom left); Lei palapalai (center); Laua'e and Hala leis (center right); Mixed fern lei with maile (bottom).

Pala'ā Fern

Lei pala'ā

Pala fern and maile

Wearing the Lei pala'ā

(From left to right) Red pūkiawe; White pūkiawe; Lei pūkiawe; Wearing the Lei pūkiawe; Lei of pūkiawe and 'ōhelo leaves.

a lei or it was combined with other materials. Quite often it was used as the binding that held the lei together. Divisions of the fronds were torn from the stem and braided to make the lei. To the braid, lehua flowers or ʻaʻaliʻi seed pods or other materials were added.

A dark stemmed form of this fern is called palai-ʻula.

PALA, MARATTIA DOUGLASII

A native fern which grows in the deep shade of the wet forest. It has become rare since it is readily eaten by wild pigs. It is a large fern with deep green, ovate fronds three or more feet long twice divided, having curious swellings at the base of the leaflets. Pala was wound with maile to bring out the maile scent and together in a lei was offered to the gods at the temples.

PALAʻĀ, PALAPALAʻĀ, LACE FERN, SPHENOMERIS CHINENSIS

One of the most common ferns of the dry forest with smooth, shiny green to brown stems. Fronds are six to 18 inches long, tough and finely dissected.

In legend, Hiʻiaka while on a mission for Pele, her sister and volcano goddess, encounters the moʻo, dragons of Puna. To protect herself from them, she wore a skirt of palaʻā about her hips and entangled the dragons with the ferns, thus defeating them and sending them on their way. Since then the women wore leis of palaʻā to dispel any and all female ailments.

LAUAʻE, MICROSORIUM SCOLOPENDRIA

A maile scented fern with lobed, broad, flat, oblong, shiny, dark green fronds much like the leaves of the breadfruit and shiny brown to black stems. Fronds grow from scaly, creeping rhizomes. Spore bearing fronds have narrower lobes than those that do not bear spores. Bits of lauaʻe were used with flowers and especially the drupes of the hala in lei making.

PŪKIAWE, ʻAʻALIʻI MAHU, MAIELE, KĀWAʻU, STYPHELIA TAMEIAMEIAE

A native shrub three to six feet tall with many small stiff, leathery, sharply tipped leaves, inconspicuous white flowers and white to red berries. The berries were added to leis for color or used by themselves.

PAʻINIU, ASTELIA SPP.

A Hawaiian lily of the wet forest. A conspicuous plant having silvery leaves and bright orange berries. Hawaiians do not remove the translucent, silvery outer layer and braid the layers into leis as is believed by some writers. Instead they stripped the silvery leaves up the center into two pieces. Each piece was looped at one end. The looped pieces were plaited together. New pieces were added at regular intervals. Other materials such as lehua blossoms, palapalai fern, sedges were sometimes added to the braid. Some sources believe that in ancient times the lei paʻiniu was made only on the island of Hawaiʻi and that it has not been until more recent times when *Astelia* other than the species *menziesiana* have been used for leis.

Like the leis of red lehua that were made on visits to the volcano, paʻiniu leis were also evidence that one had visited the area. The leis are seldom seen today.

NUKU-ʻIʻIWI, KA-ʻIʻIWI, STRONGYLODON RUBER

A long smooth vine of the dry forest with three parted leaves and inch-long bright scarlet flowers borne on long hanging spikes. Usually the stems of two spikes were tied together to make the lei nuku-ʻiʻiwi. The knot rested on the nape of the neck and each spike laid on the breasts. Sometimes, the flowers which resemble the beak of the ʻiʻiwi in shape and color were strung or woven into leis.

According to Hawaiian folk lore, red was sacred to the gods and to those who loved them. Only those who were beloved by the gods would dare to wear the lehua and nuku-'i'iwi leis "lest they be haunted by a headless woman carrying her head under her arm."

'ĀKIA, WIKSTROEMIA SPP.

A group of small trees and shrubs found growing on the leeward sea coasts of some of the islands and in the dry forests and open plains to elevations of about 4,000 feet. The bark was used for cordage and the leaves, roots, and bark of some species were pounded and used to stupefy fish in saltwater pools thus making them easier to catch. The tiny, tubular, heady scented, yellow-green flowers are four parted without petals and clustered at branch tips or leaf axils. The flowers may have been used in leis and were probably selected for their fragrance. However, it is the yellow to orange to red fruits of about one-half inch in diameter that were pierced and strung like beads in ancient times to make the necklace that is called lei 'ākia ha'a ha'a. Many strands entwined with maile made a handsome lei.

NĀNŪ, NĀ'Ū, GARDENIA BRIGHAMII, G. REMYI, G. MANNII

The native gardenias have fragrant white single flowers with five to nine petals spreading from one to two inches in diameter borne on small to large trees ranging in heights from six to forty-five feet. These endemic gardenias grow in the wet and dry forests on all the major islands.

Leis of Nānū or nā'ū were prized possessions and preferred for their fragrance. In the legend of Ka'ala and Ka'aiali'i, the women of Lāna'i presented floral tributes to Kamehameha and others when they came to Keālia for sport. The floral tributes consisted of leis of nā'ū, plaited in pili grass and wound with maile.

'ĀKULIKULI 'ŌHELO OR 'ĀKULIKULI 'AE'AE, 'ŌHELO KAI, LYCIUM SANDWICENSE

A sprawling, low endemic shrub growing to heights of two to three feet, having fleshy leaves, small white to lavender flowers and red berries found growing on limestone and lava rocks close to the sea and brackish water on the arid coasts of all the islands.

The red berries, the size of currants, were gathered and strung on lengths of fiber. The berries were selected as a lei material because of their color and their ready availability. Berries could be gathered the year around since the plant blossomed and fruited all year with a heavy period in the fall. Like so many other lei materials, the berries may have been the only functional and available lei material within the reach of the villagers living along the beaches on the lee side of the islands.

Hi'iaka and Lohi'au on the return trip to Hawai'i were greeted by women stringing leis of 'ākulikuli 'ae'ae when they arrived at Ewa on O'ahu.

'ŌHAI, SESBANIA TOMENTOSA

A low almost prostrate shrub with silvery wool covered branches and leaves and having dark orange, almost brown, and scarlet pealike inch long flowers. The 'ōhai is found growing on all the islands on the lee side, but is now a very rare plant. The pealike flowers were strung.

PUAKAUHI, 'ĀWIKIWIKI, CANAVALIA SPP.

A perennial vine with 1.5 inch long, very deep purple, pealike flowers found growing in the dry forest of all the islands. Flowers were strung as single lei material or combined, as other flowers, leaves and berries were, with other materials found in the same forest such as the red, orange, yellow, and pale green blossoms of the wiliwili *(Erythrina sandwicensis).* Most of the many native *Canavalia* were used in leis including the introduced

(From top to bottom in the left column): Kūkae-nēnē; Silver geranium; Lei pa'iniu; Mixed lei of lehua buds, pa'iniu, silver geranium, pūkiawe, kūkae-nēnē and *Hedyotis;* Wearing the Lei pa'iniu (top right); Pa'iniu (bottom right).

Lei ʻākia and ʻukiʻuki

ʻĀkia flowers (top left); ʻĀkia fruit (center left).

ʻUkiʻuki berries

A twisted lei of ʻākia fruits

Naupaka kuahiwi (top left); Lei of likolehua and pūkiawe (bottom left).

'Ākulikuli-'ae'ae—Photo by Henry Geis (top right); Nuku-'i'iwi (center right); Liko 'ōhelo (bottom right).

Māmane (top left); Lei māmane (top right); Lei of māmane, lehua, ʻaʻaliʻi, kūkae-nēnē, oa and palapalai (center); Wiliwili flowers and seeds (bottom left); Lei pua wiliwili (bottom right).

Kō (left); Wearing the Lei Kō (right).

Moa (top); ʻŌhai (below).

'Āwikiwiki—Photo by Henry Geis

species *C. carthartica.* These leis are seldom seen today.

HALA-PEPE, DRACAENA, PLEOMELE SPP.

A distinctly different shaped tree with narrow ribbon-like leaves growing in very dry to moderately moist forests. The tubular, yellow or yellow-green flowers were used in clusters and combined with other dry forest materials; or the flowers were strung lengthwise through their tubes into many strands; or the flowers were strung laterally through their tubes resembling spokes in a wheel into a lei poepoe, round lei. The hala-pepe was not a commonly used lei material even though it was sacred to Laka, but it was used by those who lived in the dry forest because it may have been the only flowers available and suitable for use.

MĀMANE, SOPHORA CHRYSOPHYLLA

A sprawling tree or erect shrub or small tree, the māmane, a native of Hawai'i, grows on all the islands except Moloka'i at altitudes of 1,000 to 9,500 feet. From January through April, trees are covered with clusters of bright yellow pea-shaped flowers. The flowers are strung one by one or attached in clusters to a central cord by winding or plaiting for the lei māmane. The lei was preferred for its color, yellow being the favorite of the ali'i.

KŌ, SUGAR CANE, SACCHARUM OFFICINARUM

A member of the grass family, the sugar cane was introduced to Hawai'i by the early Polynesian travellers and cultivated in gardens as a source of sugar. During the blooming season of November-December, the rose-lavendar-silver tassels were torn apart and the pieces plaited into the little known lei puakō. During post Cook years, natives fashioned leis from strips of the flower stalk by braiding ornate patterns. These leis were usually worn on hats made from the same fiber, braided strips of the flower stalk.

LIMU KALA, SARGASSUM SPP.

Another unusual lei said to contain magical powers was made from the limu kala, a common, tough, spinney, yellow-brown seaweed. The seaweed is easily distinguished by its hollylike spiny leaves and yellow "berries" and can be found readily along all of the islands' beaches. The seaweed gets its name from its spines.

Because kala also means "to loosen, to free," the seaweed was used in a healing and cleansing rite. A lei of limu kala was draped around the neck of a physically, emotionally or spiritually ill person who then entered the sea. As he swam, the lei floated free from about his neck, taking with it the guilt or evil that caused the illness.

Some dancers of old when performing at the ancient hula house a dance of gratitude imitating the movements of the turtle, draped themselves with the lei limu kala while other dancers would wear the lei limu kala when performing any dance associated with the sea.

The lei limu kala was and is still offered at the ku'ula by fishermen or anyone who wishes to be favored by or is grateful to the sea.

It is made by plaiting short lengths together or by knotting together longer lengths. When freshly made, lei limu kala is unusually beautiful.

The lei limu kala is the emblem of Molokini, the ninth island in size in the Hawaiian group.

Lei limu kala offering at the ku'ula (left); Gathering limu kala (top right); Lei limu kala (bottom right).

'UALA, 'UWALA, SWEET POTATO, IPOMOEA BATATAS, PŌHUEHUE, BEACH MORNING GLORY, IPOMOEA PES-CAPRAE, WAUKE, PAPER MULBERRY, BROUSSONETIA PAPYRIFERA

Leis of the 'uala and pōhuehue vines and strips of crude kapa made from the bark of the wauke were worn around the necks of new mothers and were used to slap their breasts to induce the flow of milk. The pōhuehue was said to have magical powers and was used sometimes for bewitching. Surfers in days of old would strike the ocean waters with "leis" of pōhuehue vines whenever they wished to have big waves for surfing.

Mama and Dad waited as anxiously as we did for summer to come. After the summer chores were done and we had earned enough money to buy new shoes for the next school year, Mama and Dad would pack up the family with fishing, crabbing, and camping gear and whisk us off for a week or so of living in the wilderness. Always Uncle and Aunty Afat and their family came with us. What a mess of cousins that was, I think we were sixth cousins, though as children the kinship seemed closer. When we all grew up, we discovered that what we felt as children was true, for Hawaiians believe that relationships are still close no matter how distant they may be in actuality and that family ties are not severed at third or fourth cousins, but continue, ad infinitum.

Aunty and Uncle Afat had six children, Hawaiian-Chinese on their father's side and Hawaiian-Portuguese on their mother's. Their family included Aunty Aholo, a tiny lady of regal breeding and education who was raised in the household of Hawai'i's last reigning monarch, Lili'u-o-ka-lani. Their family included also their young mischievous cousin, James, and another young man called Kealoha. When we were all there, the total was twenty-two campers.

We all piled into Uncle Afat's pineapple hauling, flatbed truck, both families and all the gear. We did not drive very far because the wilderness was closeby at Kawela.

The parents and the older kids setup camp just above the high water mark on the beach while we younger ones tied pieces of dried, salted, codfish to one end of four to five feet lengths of cord. On the other end, we tied pieces of driftwood which served as floats. All this we did in preparation for catching crabs. We ate half of the cod before we even set it out for bait.

The bait set, we walked up the beach for a swim while we waited for the crabs to take the bait. For the rest of the day we swam, scooped up the crabs that took our bait, rolled around in the warm sand, sucked on oranges and lollipops both of which were special treats for us, explored the beach, laughed and caroused around.

When evening came, the mothers and older girls cooked dinner over a kiawe wood fire while the fathers and the older boys laid the surround net in the calm evening waters. They left the net. It would remain there throughout the night.

We ate a hearty meal. The salt air, the sunshine, the kiawe wood fire and the day's activities had increased our appetites many times over. It gets dark. The stars hang close to us, so big, so bright, so quiet. The spell of the night is broken by stray pigs and cows that nudge at our food stores, clang and clatter our pots, munch our oranges and dip into our poi.

Early the next morning, we are awakened and sent to gather pōhuehue vines. We find them. They cover the beaches just above the high water mark. Then, with vines in hand, we slowly enter the cold morning waters. Our fathers call softly, "pa'ipa'i" and with leis of pōhuehue, we slap and agitate the water sending all the fish into the net that was set out the night before. "Pa'ipa'i" the fathers call again and the waters we slap become rough and choppy as we shoo the fish into the net. What a marvelous way to greet a new day!

IPU, HUE, PŌHUE, GOURD, LAGENARIA SICERARIA

In an account of "Religious Observances in Relation to Children," David Malo describes an unusual lei consisting of a gourd suspended on a cord around the neck of an image of Lono (god of all growing things) in the mua, men's shrine. The gourd contained dried 'awa root and the ear of a pig that was offered or fed to the deity to insure the gods' favor upon the boy child who was being inducted into manhood. The ceremony marked the end of the boy's eating with his mother and other females.

The placement of the pig's ear into the gourd and the offering of bananas, coconuts, and 'awa at the altar were accompanied by a pule ipu, a gourd prayer, to Lono in which the father prays that his son be blessed with vigor and strength such as that of the gourd vine.

The prayer completed, the father sucks on the 'awa root, drinks the 'awa, eats the food prepared for the ceremony and declares the boy installed into the society of manhood. The ceremony ends with a feast of pork and vegetables.

The gourd lei served another purpose in ancient Hawai'i, that of marking a kauwā, branded servant, slave, for sacrifice at the war temple. A slave was selected from the slave reservation. If he was not to be sacrificed immediately, he was marked with "a garland of waiting," lei i ka 'olo, a gourd suspended on a cord.

There may be a kinship of the two gourd leis. They both served as marks for the gods—one for Lono, god of peace and fructification and one for Kū, god of war.

LIMU PAHAPAHA, PALAHAPALAHA, ULVA FASCIATA

Another seaweed lei was made of strands of pahapaha plaited together to show that one has been to Polihale, Kaua'i.

Limu pahapaha was one of the few seaweeds that the Hawaiians kept indefinitely by drying. This may have been the original reason for bringing it back from Polihale. Hawaiians would collect the seaweed on the reef at low tide when the ocean was calm. They would plait the strands of seaweed, carry home the leis of limu around their necks, then hang them out to dry to be used later when they pounded it and mixed it with water making a poultice for bruises.

Some believe that the lei limu pahapaha was used in the same way as the lei limu kala.

OTHER TEMPORARY MATERIALS

It is not unreasonable to assume that other floral materials may have been used by the early Hawaiians in their leis even though records of their use are non-existent or sparse. These were fresh, temporary materials that lend themselves to the lei making techniques, materials that were readily available and abundant and materials that could have filled the Hawaiians' needs and reasons for making and wearing a lei. Some fragrant, while others have interesting texture and color. Like the Hawaiians of today, it is possible that the Hawaiians of old were just as fascinated by these materials and just as desirous of carrying and keeping them as momenta of a visit to the mountains or uninhabited seashores or far reaches of the deep valleys.

These materials were: the heady scented pua-pilo *(Capparis sandwichiana);* 'ākia *(Wikstroemia)* flowers and leaves; the silvery 'āhinahina *(Geranium cuneatum)* leaves and flowers; the flower clusters of the 'iliahi *(Santalum);* the brilliant young pink leaves and the berries of the 'ōhelo *(Vaccinium);* the white beautifully scented flowers of the *Hedyotis fluviatilis,* alahe'e *(Canthium odoratum),* kūpaoa or na'ena'e *(Dubautia),* and the naupaka *(Scaevola);* the red-orange and creamy yellow flowers of the wiliwili *(Erythrina);* the white flowers and berries of the 'ūlei *(Osteomeles anthyllidifolia);* the yellow flowers of the po'olānui *(Bidens cosmoides),* the nehe *(Lipochaeta)* and the kolomona *(Cassia gaudichaudii);* the fragrant white kamani flowers *(Calophyllum inophyllum)*; the flowers of the hau *(Hibiscus tiliaceus)* and aloalo *(Hibiscus)*; the yellow-orange flowers and fruit of the kāmakahala *(Labordia)*; the black, shiny fruit of the kūkae-nēnē, 'ai a ka nēnē *(Coprosma ernodeoides)*; the clusters of blue flowers of the pōhinahina, kolokolo-kahakai *(Vitex ovata)*; the delicately fragrant flowers of the kolokolo-kuahiwi *(Lysimachia)*; flowers of the endemic lobilias, in particular, the papaya-like flowers of the 'ōhā wai *(Clermontia grandiflora)*; the tubular, yellow flowers of the 'aiea *(Nothocestrum latifolium)*, a dry forest tree; the pink to red flowers of the uhiuhi *(Mezoneuron kavaiense)*; the blue berries of the 'uki'uki *(Dianella)*; various ferns, mosses and blossoming grasses.

Six basic methods were used to construct the temporary leis of ancient Hawai'i making it possible to use almost any material. The haku lei or lei maker, chose the method that was most appropriate for the materials that were available and most suitable for her needs. Thus, a lei of 'ilima ku-kahakai in Ka'ū may have been strung on the stringy fibers of the pandanus aerial roots, while the 'ilima ku-kula of Waimea was strung on the stems of blossoming grasses and the 'ilima-lei cultivated in lowland housing compounds was strung on lengths of hau *(Hibiscus tiliaceus)* bast. The availability of materials resulted in the use of different binding materials also. If the materials were gathered in the mountains and the leis constructed there, then perhaps they were arranged in a braid of ferns, or they could have been carried home in tī leaf packages where the lei was made by attaching the materials to a center cord of banana with a wrapping string of hau bast. The availability of materials resulted in the use of different methods of construction too.

KĪPU'U, (HĪPU'U, NĪPU'U), the knotting method. Leaf stems or short vine lengths were knotted together to make a length long enough to circle the head or drape around the neck as in the lei 'ōlapa, lei lapalapa and lei maile. A binding thread was not needed. The maile was first prepared by a process called, 'u'u, stripping, i.e. removing the bark from the woody stem.

HILI, (HILO), the braiding, plaiting method. The term applied only to the braiding of a single material. A binding thread was not used. Constructed by this method were lei palapalai, lei pala'ā, lei pa'iniu, lei limu pahapaha and sometimes lei maile when three or more lengths were used. Paliting three strands was used most often.

HAKU, the arrange-in-a-braid method. The construction method in which flowers, leaves and fruits with stems of two to three inches were added to a three-strand plait of ferns, dried banana stalk skin, hau bast or tī leaves. Materials with supple, tough stems were best suited for this technique, since they too, became a part of the braid.

WILI, the winding method. Materials were cut with stems one to three inches long. The stems were tied to a center cord of ferns, dried banana stalk skin, hau bast or tī leaves or were tied together without the center cord with a string of hau or banana. The tying consisted of winding the string around the center cord and stems two or more times. The wili method of construction may consist of simply twisting two or more strands of material together as in the lei kauna'oa and sometimes the lei maile. Knotting was not necessary until the lei was completed. In addition to all the materials that were used in the haku method, flowers, leaves and fruits with somewhat shorter and more brittle stems were also suitable for this technique.

KUI, the stringing method. The material was pierced with a needle (mānai) through the center or side and held together by a single string. The method was simple, but frequently time consuming. Metal needles were not known in ancient Hawai'i; instead, one fashioned from the coconut nī'au, (midrib of the coconut leaf), or stems from flowers of native grasses was used. The string was hau bast. Sometimes, 'ilima was strung on the thin, stringy fiber from the aerial roots of the pandanus. Straight stringing, lengthwise through the centers of the flowers was called kui pololei. Round stringing, crosswise through the stems or ovaries of flowers and arranging as spokes in a wheel was called kui poepoe. Flat stringing, crosswise through the stems or ovaries of the flowers and arranging them alternating from side to side of the string, as in the lei maunaloa, is called kui lau (leaf). So a lei strung straight is called lei pololei, one strung round is called lei poepoe and one strung with blossoms alternating from side to side is called lei lau. Lei 'ilima, lei kou, lei hala, and lei mokihana are kui pololei.

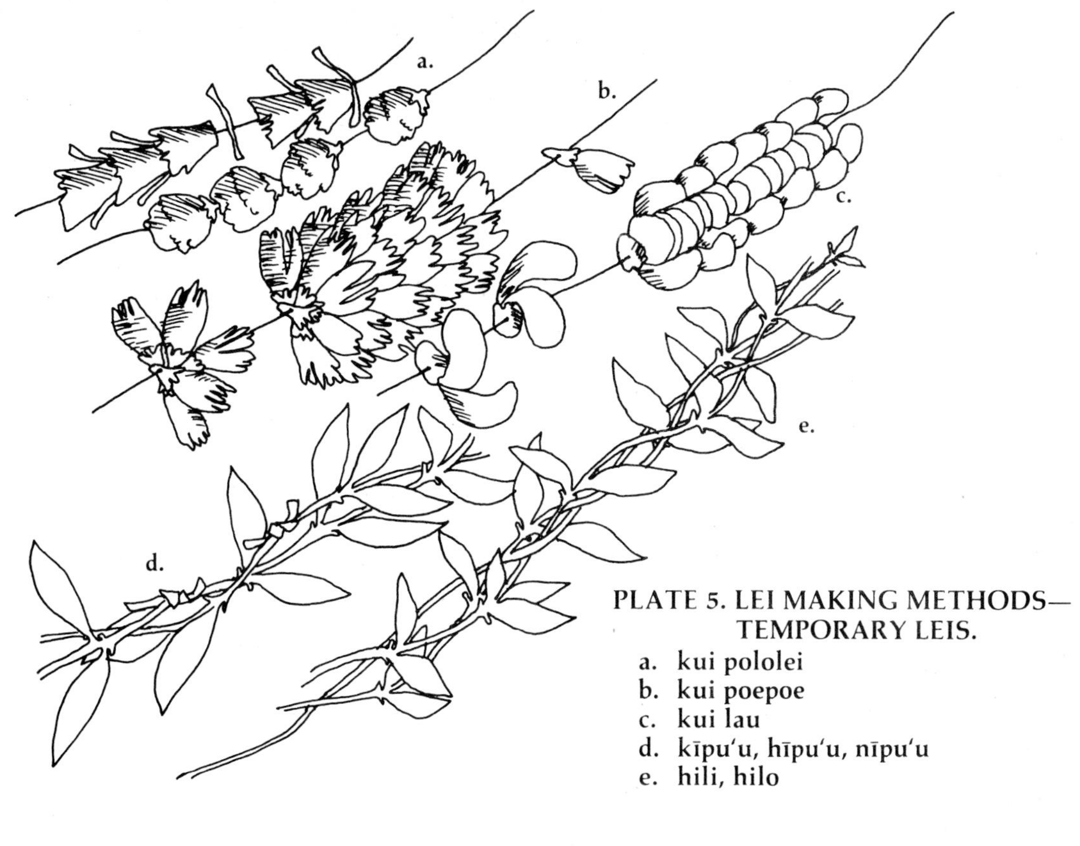

PLATE 5. LEI MAKING METHODS—TEMPORARY LEIS.

a. kui pololei
b. kui poepoe
c. kui lau
d. kīpuʻu, hīpuʻu, nīpuʻu
e. hili, hilo

PLATE 6. DETAIL OF LEI MAKING METHODS.

a. kīpuʻu, hīpuʻu, nīpuʻu
b. hili, hilo

PLATE 5. LEI MAKING METHODS—TEMPORARY LEIS. (continued)
f, h. wili
g. haku
i. **humu-papa, kui papa**

HUMU-PAPA, (KUI PAPA), the sew-to-a-foundation method. Floral material with or without stems, was sewn to a foundation of dried banana stalk skin, pandanus, coconut or tī leaves or other such materials. The humu-papa method was a comfortable one for head leis.

(See illustration, plates 5, 6 page 69, 70).

LEI PACKAGES

Leis of temporary materials were stored and carried about in tī leaf packages called pū'olo lā'ī or narrow banana stalk trays called hā mai'a. Leis of permanent materials were wrapped in soft kapa and stored in covered containers called 'umeke pōhue and 'umeke lā'au. In post Cook times after the introduction of tobacco, feather leis were stored in tobacco tins with bits of tobacco. In contemporary times, they are still stored with tobacco to ward off insects that may ruin the leis.

The pū'olo lā'ī and the ha mai'a are still to this day the best way to store and carry fresh leis about. The cool tī leaves and cool banana stalk keep flowers, leaves, seeds and ferns from drying and withering, and from being crushed and bruised.

There are several ways for making a pū'olo lā'ī. A large lei is wrapped in a package made with eight to twelve leaves. The number depends on the size of the leaves. The leaves are left attached to the stalk or they may be removed from the stalk and tied together around the stems with a wet, dried leaf or some other tying fiber. The bunch of leaves is turned with stalk or stem end up. The lei is wound around the stalk or stem and is held in place by drawing up one leaf by its tip and holding it in place at the stalk or stem. All other leaves are drawn up to the stalk or stem and held in place until the lei is completely covered, then the leaf tips are tied securely with a half a leaf stripped lengthwise, or with a wet, dried leaf, or with some other tying fiber. The package is carried by the stem end or by the young unfurled leaf.

Smaller leis are wrapped in packages made with five to ten tī leaves, again depending on the size of the leaves. The lei is placed lengthwise on one leaf. Other leaves are placed with stems alternating from one end to the other end and covering the lei. Stems and tips of leaves are gathered up at both ends of the bundle and tied securely.

The smallest leis are wrapped in two tī leaves. The midribs of the leaves are first removed. The lei is rolled into a tight, small heap then placed on one leaf at the tip end. The lei is rolled into the leaf with the stem making the final turn. The bundle is then placed on the second leaf with the open ends of the bundle facing the tip and stem. The bundle is rolled up into the second leaf to the stem, then the stem is split, the ends knotted together at a point close to the leaf and drawn around the bundle in opposite directions and finally tied together to secure the package. (see illustration, plate 7, page 72).

The banana stalk tray or hā mai'a is made by first cutting down the whole banana stalk or tree, removing the leaf and fruit end and finally cutting the stalk into lei lengths. The outside layers of skin are removed and cast aside. The remaining layers, except for the very center ones, are pulled free and used as trays for carrying and storing leis. (see illustration, plate 8, page 73).

We learned to make leis by watching and helping Mama as she strung the blossoms or attached them to banana fiber with a binding thread of the same material. She never gave us a formal lesson and I am certain that we never asked for one or questioned her since we always knew that the answer would be, "don't niele" (don't ask frivolous questions). So we watched and helped and learned.

While we were children, we made many leis. We pierced pukanawila (bougainvillea), pua kalaunu (crownflower), pīkake, (jasmine) and 'ōkole-'oi'oi (marigold). We braided gingers with pala'ā

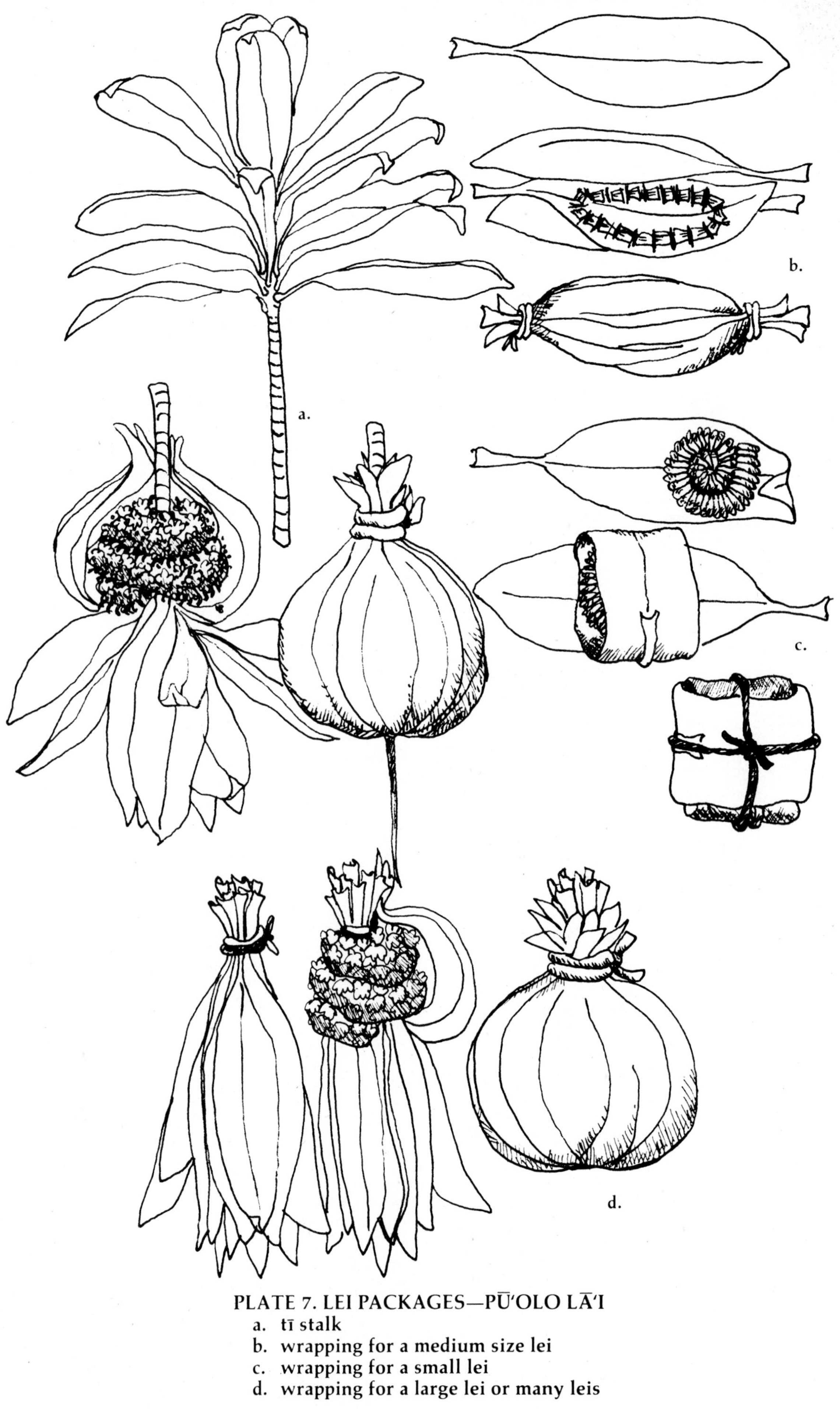

PLATE 7. LEI PACKAGES—PŪʻOLO LĀʻI
a. tī stalk
b. wrapping for a medium size lei
c. wrapping for a small lei
d. wrapping for a large lei or many leis

PLATE 8. LEI PACKAGES—HĀ MAIʻA

fern and attached pua ahiahi (four o'clock flowers), ageratums and Boston fern to long strips of banana fiber with a binding thread. But when we were sent off to school in Honolulu and to college on the mainland, we made fewer leis and temporarily lost the touch for lei making. We were too busy being educated. We purchased the leis that we needed for our favorite football player and date, for the song contests, for the proms, for the hellos and the goodbyes.

A renewed interest in the art of lei making occurred when I went to work for the Department of Parks and Recreation in Honolulu in 1952 and became a part of a small group of recreation professionals who were interested in preserving and re-vitalizing the arts of Hawai'i—the music, the dance, the poetry and the legends, the visual arts and crafts. In the group was one who would become a close friend, 'Āina Keawe.

'Āina and I worked with children. Together we taught a group of them to make some leis for the Annual Lei Contest in Honolulu. It was our first experience with teaching the children to use the wili method of lei making which I vaguely remembered from my childhood. We had visions of winning all of the prizes at the contest and especially the Mayor's Grand Prize of fifty dollars.

We gathered up all the lei making material we could find in Ala Moana Park—figs from the banyan trees, clusters of tiny buds from the palm trees, mock orange leaves and fruits, white star shaped blossoms from the thorny carissa bushes and a lot of other material that proved to be too difficult to handle. We set to work with our children of six through fourteen years old. The leis kept falling apart. We salvaged them by tying the broken pieces together with florist wire.

When the judging for the contest was completed, we were heartbroken. Our children had not won any of the prizes.

Some years later, 'Āina and I became involved in the management and staging of that same contest. By then, we had become skilled leimakers and were better equipped to teach the children the art of lei making. In revising the rules of the contest, we added "no wire shall be used in the leis" for we had discovered that our clever Hawaiian ancestors had created such wondrous masterpieces without it. We chuckled to ourselves then and as we always do when we remember those marvelous days of discovery and re-discovery.

THE LEI IN DANCE, MUSIC, POETRY AND LORE

The use of fresh natural material leis; their fragrance, color, texture and mobility intensified the impact of the hula ritual.

Almost every ceremony in the ritual of the hula was observed with the offering or wearing of the lei. The hālau hula, the house or temple, where the dancers received their training and practiced their art; the kuahu, the altar on which was placed an uncarved block of wood from the sacred lama *(Diospyros)* tree wrapped in 'ōlena *(Curcuma domestica,* turmeric), yellow tapa, bark cloth, representing Laka or Kapo the patron deity of the dance; the visitors; and the dancers themselves were decorated with flowers, leaves and fruits from the forest. Leis of maile, lehua, hau, 'ilima, palapalai and other native ferns; branches from the hala-pepe *(Pleomele aurea),* the 'ie'ie *(Freycinetia arborea),* the kī *(Cordyline terminalis);* fronds from the 'ekaha hāpu'u *(Asplenium nidus),* hāpu'u *(Cibotium splendens),* pala and other ferns; fruits from the ulu *(Artocarpus communis,* breadfruit), the mai'a *(Musa xparadisiaca,* banana) and the 'ōhi'a 'ai *(Eugenia malaccensis,* mountain apple); and blossoms of the hau decorated the hālau, were offered at the kuahu, or were worn by the dancers.

Strict adherence to the ceremony was observed for every aspect of the hula from the building of the hālau, the gathering of the greens, the decorating of the temple and kuahu, the dressing, debut and graduation of the dancers, to the performances for an audience. For each rite there was a special prayer, chant or song. Nathaniel B. Emerson in Unwritten Literature of Hawai'i recorded the following song-prayer, recited while gathering materials from the forest and while decorating the hālau.

"Haki pu o ka nahelehele
Haki hana maile o ka wao,
Hooulu lei ou, o Laka, e!
O Hi'iaka ke kaula nana e hooulu na ma'i,
A aeae a ulu a noho i kou kuahu,
Eia ka pule la, he pule ola,
He noi ola nou, e-e!
Chorus:
E ola ia makou, aohe hala!

This spoil and rape of the wildwood,
This plucking of wilderness maile—
Collect of garlands, Laka, for you.
Hi'iaka, the prophet, heals our diseases.
Enter, possess, inspire your altar;
Heed our prayer, 'tis for life;
Our petition for you is for life.
Chorus:
Give us life, safe from transgression!"

The simplest hula chores were not devoid of ritual. One beautiful rite which is seldom enacted by present day dancers is the ceremony of dressing for a performance. In preparation for a performance, the hālau becomes a common dressing area for both men and women dancers. The kumu-hula, dance master, takes charge and with proper ceremony announces the dressing ceremony. Protocol dictates that the first articles of dress are the anklets. The dancers move together in unison. The dressing routine becomes a dance. The adornment of each article is accompanied by a mele, song—one for the kupe'e, anklets; one for the pā'ū, skirt; and one for the leis.

As the dancers knot the leis about head and neck, they sing this song recorded by N.B. Emerson in Unwritten Literature of Hawai'i.

"Ke lei mai la o Ka-ula i ke kai, e!
Ke malamalama o Ni'ihau, ua malie.
A malie, ua pa ka Inu-wai.
Ke inu mai la na hala o Naue i ke kai.
No naue, ka hala, no Puna ka wahine.
No ka lua i Kilauea.

Ka-ula wreaths her brow with the ocean
Ni'ihau shines forth in the calm.
After the calm blows the wind Inu-wai;
Naue's palms then drink in the salt.
From Naue the palm, from Puna, the woman—
Aye, from the pit, Kilauea."

It is the lei that unites the dancer with the patron deity of the hula. Through the lei, the dancer is inspired to perform magnificently for the lei is kino lau (a form) of Laka herself. The lei dedicated to Laka was kapu, reserved for Laka and the dancer, could not be given to another nor covered with other leis.

A visitor to the hālau also took part in the ceremonies of the hula. Upon entering the hālau, he offered prayers of admiration and praise at the altar while presenting leis that were favored by Laka. Leis of maile, palapalai, 'ilima, lehua blossoms.

". . . Behold, the lehua blooms of Kaana
The women are stringing enough to enwreath goddess Kapo . . ."

He asked for her blessings, for self, for dancers, for teacher, for others present and for the lei.

". . . Oh Laka make beautiful the lei;
Inspire the dancers when they stand before the assembly."

Since it was the telling of the story and the singing of praises with body movement that was the important thing in the hula, the dancers were careful not to over-adorn themselves. The "words" of the story were not muffled by an excessive number of leis. One for the head and one for the neck were sufficient for enhancing the storytelling.

Because the hula was an art form in which the ali'i was actively engaged, some of the dancers performed with the leis that denoted their breeding and station in society—the lei palaoa and the lei hulu manu. Well known accounts of dancers wearing the lei palaoa and the lei hulu manu were recorded by early explorers and visitors to Hawai'i not only with written word but with illustrations by artists who accompanied them.

When we were children we had a kumu hula. She was an excessive woman, size-wise, strength-wise, mirth-wise, and warmth-wise. She was well trained in the art of the hula and she wanted all five girls in the Adams family to be the same way. She drilled us, massaged us, scolded us and drilled us again.

Usually all five of us, Aineiki, Hester, Jo, Irma and I, would go across town to the kumu hula's house for our weekly lesson. Sometimes Mama would go with us for she helped to interpret some of the old meles. Sometimes Hester did not go with us for she spent most of the year in school at Honolulu. Aineiki and Jo loved the lessons and became beautiful dancers. Hester stumbled a lot. Irma and I would rather climb the mango trees which we did, when we ran away from the lessons. Besides, I was too skinny, too tall, and too awkward. I could never be the graceful, agile and supple person that was the dancer. And I never was, though in later years, I longed to be that person.

Many years passed and I became acquainted with another kumu hula. This one taught many children to dance at Honolulu playgrounds. We became friends and I mustered up enough courage to ask her if she thought that I could learn to do the hula. Without looking up from the lei humupapa of yellow pompom chrysanthemums and fern that she was showing me how to do, she replied, "You are very talented already. You don't need any more talents." Though she said it gruffly and abruptly, she meant to be gentle and complimentary, for this was the way of my friend, kumu hula Alice Namakelua, who was my kumu lei humupapa.

In ancient Hawaiian lore, the lei was a favorite token of the gods and goddesses. Pele favored the lei lehua. Laka chose the lei maile when she was docile and as Kapo, the lei hala when she was angry. Kukuena, Laka's mother and Pele's elder sister, preferred the lei 'ilima and presided over the making and distribution of leis. Hiku, goddess of love wore skirts of leis.

Kukuena gave the beautiful, ill-fated Hōpoe, Hi'iaka's friend, a grove of lehua trees and taught her the art of lei making with the lehua blossoms. Hōpoe danced with the garlands of lehua. Soon she taught Hi'iaka the art of the hula. Since then, the hula and the lei have become inseparable.

Mai-u'u and Ma-a'a, goddesses of the wilderness, who were responsible for making the leis and decorating the superior gods with them, were called upon by Hi'iaka as she prayed for the restoration of Lohi'au.

Leis were offered as tokens of love, homage, and appeasement to the akua, the great gods, at the heiau, temples, and to the 'aumakua, the family gods at their kuahu, altar. Stewart, in his book Journey Through The Sandwich Islands, described a pile of rubble at Hale o Keawe within the City of Refuge at Honaunau as, "A large pile of broken calabashes and cocoanut shells lay in the centre, and a considerable heap of dried and partly rotten wreaths of flowers, branches of shrubs and bushes, and fragments of tapa, (the accumulated offerings of former days), formed an unsightly mound immediately before each of the images."

Fragrant plant materials were preferred. Yellow and red were favored colors. Kāne, the great god, preferred yellow over red; for all the other gods, red was sacred.

Visitors to Ke-ana-o-Hina, the cave of Hina, on Moloka'i left gifts of leis. Women visitors wore a tī leaf protection.

Leis were offered to the shark god. Ka'ahupāhau and her brother, Ka-hi'u-kā, shark 'aumakua of Pearl Harbor, favored the lei 'ilima. Ka'ahupāhau devoured the chiefess Papio because the chiefess was impertinent to her caretaker who had scolded the woman for wearing 'ilima leis while swimming in the lagoon.

Haumea, the earth mother goddess, the great source of female fertility who presided over childbirth; wife of Wākea, said to be the mother of the Pele sisters, wore leis of tī about her head and neck.

In ancient as well as in present day Hawaiian poetry and song, the lei sometimes takes on a figurative meaning. This is not unusual since in poetry the world over a single word, a line, a verse, an entire poem usually is a figurative expression rather than a literal one. These figurative expressions appear in Hawaiian prose, all to the confusion of a novice of the Hawaiian language.

In a description of the birth rites of a royal son, David Malo in his Hawaiian Antiquities, writes the following:

"... but if a boy, it was carried to the heiau, there to have the naval string cut in a ceremonious fashion... Thereupon, he applied the bamboo edge and severed the cord; and, having sponged the wound to remove the blood (kupenu), with a pledget of soft olonā fibre, ʻoloa, the kahuna prayed:

Kupenu ula;
Kupenu lei;
Kumu lei.
Aka halapa i ke akua i laau wai la.

Cleanse the red blood from the stump;
Cleanse it from the cord;
Bind up the cord.
It is for the god to safeguard this child,
to make him flourish like a well
watered plant."

This poetic statement says much more than what appears in Malo's translation. Further examination of the words bring to light a deeper, more profound and more stirring meaning. A meaning which clearly defines the Hawaiians' regard for the lei.

The umbilical cord in this instance is referred to as "lei" not the usual "piko," navel cord, or "kaula," or "aho" and for good reason. It is this cord that transmits life and love to the embryo. It is this lei that gives food, breath, warmth and love of mother and father to the unborn child. The child so filled with life and love is, even after birth, referred to lovingly as "lei." The favorite child, punahele, is often carried about with arms encircling the neck of the bearer. This, too, enforces the Hawaiians' symbolic use of "lei" meaning beloved child. Pregnant women avoided wearing a lei with ends tied together and forming a circle fearing strangulation of the unborn child.

This fragment from a mele inoa, a name song, composed in honor of Līloa, later passed down to ʻUmi and then to Kalani-nui-a-mamao is another illustration of figurative expression which poetically describes Līloa as a beloved one of great strength.

"O ke kulei ula oe;

A garland of red flowers thou;"

The red flowers are the lehua, a symbol of strength.

The lei was synonymous with love and love-making. Hawaiian poetic phrases which express the desire for a lei, the caressing and fondling of a lei, the evening lei, the taking of a lei, all deal with love and love-making. An early example of this synonymity is to be found in the Myth of Pele and Hiʻiaka. Prince Lohiʻau confesses his love for Hiʻiaka at the court of Pele-ula in Kou (Honolulu) while engaged in a contest of the hula kilu with this song:

"A ka lihi au i ka hala o Hanalei;
Lei au i ka hala o Poʻoku e, eia oe.
He ku oe naʻu, e ke aloha;
Ina oe maloko e, eia oe."

"I neighbor the land of the wreath,
My luck to pine for a pandanus crown.
Oh wouldst thou but entwine the wreath,
love
Admit to the shrine of thy heart."

The poetic figurative prose expressions of later periods still adhere to the traditions of these synonymies: the lei, referring to a child, a loved one; the lei, referring to love and love-making. There are also those that simply sing the praises of a beautiful wreath.

"Ku'u pua i li'a ai
A'u i kui a lawa
I lei ho'oiehie
Nō ke ano ahiahi.
HUI
Ahi wela mai nei loko
I ka hana a ke aloha
E lalawe nei ku'u kino
Konikoni lua i ka pō nei.

My flower desired
For me to braid and bind
An elegant lei
For evening time.
CHORUS
Hot fire here within
The act of love
Overpowers my body
Throbbing last night."

From "Ka Makani Kā'ili Aloha," a song composed by Matthew H. Kāne, expressing a longing of a husband for a wife who has deserted him.

"HUI
Ku'u pua, Ku'u lei, Ku'u milimili e,
Ku'u lei kau i ka wēkiu
A he milimili 'oe, a he hiwahiwa na'u
A he lei mau nō ku'u kino.
CHORUS
My flower, my lei, my toy
My lei placed supreme,
You my toy, my pride,
A lei forever for my body."

From a song, KA MOA'E, by
Solomon Hiram.

E lei aku 'oe i ku'u aloha
I ko'olua nou i kahi mehameha.

Wear my love as a lei
And as your companion in lonely places.

From "Ku'u Lei," a name song composed by Mary Kawena Pukui for her grandson, a beloved child, these lines:

"Haku 'ia ku'u lei
E nā lima no'eau
A wili 'ia ke aloha na'u e lei.
Pulama iho au a hi'ipoi mau
I ku'u wehi nani e lei mau nei.

My lei is woven
By skillful hands
Interwoven with love for me to wear as a lei.
I cherish and hold forever
My beautiful ornament to be worn forever as a lei.

When I was born, my great grandmother was there. I don't remember my great grandma Emelia who rocked and lulled to sleep the first six children in our family with special lullabys which she composed on the spot—a different one for each child. I don't remember the little woman in the koa rocking chair who sang for John,

Kilipi, lipi o pepe
Keone pulu
'Ohi au e.

(Emelia Hawaiianized the English words as
many Hawaiians did in her time).
(Great grandma's endearing name for John
who probably always wet).

Sleep, sleep baby
Wet John
I gather (you up).

I don't remember this grand matriarch who made sure that her great grand children were properly named in the Hawaiian tradition even though she encouraged her grand children to give them haole first names and to teach them to speak without flaw the language she never learned and never wanted to learn, so that they would be prepared to compete and survive in their Hawai'i during the time of the great haole influence. I don't remember this woman, this descendant for whom and by whom I was named. I don't remember this tūtū who gathered me up and lulled me to sleep perhaps with

Emelia, Leilehua
Pani i kou maka
E moe, e moe.

Emelia, Leilehua
Close your eyes
Sleep, sleep.

It was not until I had been sent off to school in Honolulu and had attended my first funeral that I had begun to get acquainted with her.

Some of the kids at Kamehameha could trace their families back to pre-Cook times and others boasted of twenty or thirty letter Hawaiian names which commemorated their births. Although beautiful, I thought my name was commonplace since I had translated it to mean wreath of lehua blossoms. I was such a kua'āina (a country hick) from Moloka'i even though I spoke "standard English." I was such a kua'āina, I thought then because I had never even been to a funeral, though later I discovered that I wasn't. It was a city trait to never have gone to a funeral.

My mother came to school one day, that first year at Kamehameha, to get my sister Jo and me. She took us to Haleiwa to attend the funeral of Aunty Hale. I wore my best dress, a red and white dotted swiss with a red grosgrain sash. Uncle Konohiki drove us there. The wailing could be heard as we approached the frame house, in need of paint, with a veranda across the entire front. I could not understand then what followed. Easy moving, flowing ladies in white dresses greeted first, my mother, and then Jo and me, with kisses and tears wailing "auwē, auwē" and, "this is Kiopini, auwē and Emelia, auwē." We stayed close to Mama. This was all very strange. I looked at the lady in the white casket which was draped with crownflower, ginger, carnation and maile leis. She was so young. She was so beautiful. She looked like my mother. This was Aunty Hale and all the easy moving, flowing ladies in white dresses were aunties and older cousins. The little man who sat in a straight back chair next to and at the head of the casket was Uncle Pedro. I didn't know this then, but I was determined to know.

So on my first vacation from school, at Christmastime, I bombarded my mother and father with questions and for once, they didn't hush me or discourage me from asking them. It was then that I got to know my great grandma Emelia, all my aunties and uncles and all my cousins on both sides of the family—the Scotch, Irish, Pennsylvania-Dutch side and the Hale'iwa-Hawaiian side. It was during this first vacation from school that I discovered how appropriate, how poetic and how beautiful my name and those of my brothers and sisters were.

Great grandma Emelia named me Leilehua—lehua, poetic for strength and lei, poetic for child. In the tradition of Hawaiian names, mine is appropriate. It commemorates my birth and the circumstances surrounding it. My twin brother was stillborn and I the strong child. I, Marie Emelia Leilehua Adams, swelled with pride when I returned to Kamehameha to boast of my heritage.

In the mid years of my life, a stranger on the island of Hawai'i watched as I demonstrated the various methods of lei making, he said to me, "'O wai kou inoa ma ka 'ōlelo Hawai'i?" I replied, "'O Leilehua ko'u inoa. No ke aha?" My Hawaiian was embarrassingly poor and I am sure that he sensed this, for he answered in the kind of English my mother spoke, "the lei expert." "No" said I, "the strong child," "that too" he continued, "and perhaps a wreath of lehua blossoms?" "Yes," I smiled and thought, "I love you name. Whichever way you are, you are beautiful and you are me. Mahalo no iā 'oe, e Kupuna wahine kuakahi."

LEIS OF THE CONTEMPORARY PERIOD

With the discovery of the Hawaiian Islands by western man and the introduction of new materials, natural as well as man-made, the Hawaiian lei and the traditions associated with it changed as did the needs and lifestyle of the people. Captain James Cook started the changes when he discovered the islands in 1778 during his third voyage into the Pacific. He anchored off Waimea, Kaua'i and on the morning of January 20, 1778 the first Englishman walked upon Hawaiian soil. It is possible that these may not have been the first foreigners to have found Hawai'i. Though there is no proof that others came before Cook, there is the claim that Spanish galleons sailing the Pacific from Acapulco to Manila may have stopped at Hawai'i, after the unproven discovery of the islands by the Spanish navigator Juan Gaetano in 1555.

If Spanish galleons had stopped here before Cook's arrival, this may substantiate the claims of some Hawaiians who believe that such plant and lei materials as hala-kahiki or pineapple *(Ananas cosmosus)*, hē'ī or papaya *(Carica papaya)*, kīkānia-lei *(Solanum aculeatissimum)*, pūkāmole *(Lythrum maritimum)*, and nani ahiahi or four o'clock *(Mirabilis jalapa)*, all South or Central American in origin, were here before Cook's discovery and were used in some localities for leis. Records show that Cook planted pineapple seeds which he brought from Brazil, in Tahiti in 1769. It is assumed that the pineapple was introduced to Hawai'i from Tahiti thus the Hawaiian name, "hala kahiki," pandanus from Tahiti. Cook himself may have introduced it or it may have been introduced some years later by Vancouver. Yet there are many Hawaiians who will insist that the pineapple was to be found in such places as Ka'u on Hawai'i and Ni'ihau before Cook's arrival and that the name by which they called it meant "foreign pandanus" and not "Tahiti pandanus."

There is also the mystery of the sweet potato which is an older introduction. Some believe that it was brought to Hawai'i by early Polynesian travellers from the Marquesan and Society Islands. The sweet potato is said to have originated in South America and was distributed throughout Polynesia in pre-Columbian times by Indians from the continent or by Polynesians who had been to the continent and had returned with the sweet potato as a momento of their having been there. Could this have not happened to tubers, cuttings, and seeds of other plants?

Nevertheless, dating the arrival of new plants and man-made materials to the Islands before the time of written record and even during the times of written record is sometimes impossible and may prove to be an interesting undertaking for someone. Some facts are available while others remain to be uncovered. For others, we must draw upon related historical facts and make logical assumptions.

Cook may be credited for introducing the first lei haole, foreign necklace, when on his arrival he bartered with the natives for food and water. In exchange, he gave them ". . . . nails, spikes, other iron articles, beads and mirrors . . . ." Whether these first beaded necklaces were ivory, glass, ceramic, wood or semi-precious stones is not known. Whatever they were, coupled with the introduction of iron articles and a view of another lifestyle, the change in the lei had begun.

In 1786 London merchants sent Captains Portlock and Dixon to set up trade stations in the Pacific between North America and China. The Islands made a good stopping over place for refurbishing the ships' provisions. The English ships stopped in Hawai'i on their way to the Pacific Northwest and took on stores of food and water. In the Northwest, they bartered for furs for trade with China. On their return across the Pacific, they stopped again at Hawai'i where they took on cargoes of sandalwood and left, among other things, walrus ivory from which the Hawaiians made the pendants and beads for their lei palaoa. On their return trips from China, they left silks and brocades which the Hawaiians eventually used in their lei making, first as the central cord to which they attached with silk thread, the tiny feathers for their lei hulu, then later as the lei material itself.

Subsequent voyagers and traders introduced other materials and ideas which effected changes in the lei. Don Francisco de Paulo Marin arrived in the islands in 1791. In later years he was responsible for propagating many of the newly introduced plant materials, among them the mamo or safflower, *(Carthamus tinctorius)*, and the lokelani *(Rosa damascena)*.

Captain George Vancouver during the years 1792-94 passed out to the natives packets of food plant seeds. He introduced beef cattle, goats, sheep and geese. (Captain Cook's earlier introduction of goats to Ni'ihau had all been killed before Vancouver's arrival). All of which helped to destroy the native forests, the source of supply for much of the materials used in the temporary and permanent leis. Archibald Menzies, naturalist-surgeon with Vancouver probably introduced the first orange trees, blossoms of which were used in leis, grapes and many garden vegetables.

Early Europeans and Chinese travellers and traders involved in the China trade introduced plant materials from Asia and especially southern China. Many of them ended up in the gardens of Don Francisco de Paulo Marin.

While Kamehameha I ruled the island kingdom, the old ways remained intact. The techniques of war had changed with the introduction of guns, gun powder, gunboats and iron tools. Trade and contact with the rest of the world was ever increasing, but domestic affairs, religion and politics were unchanged since Kamehameha was a devout believer and appeaser of the ancient gods.

In 1819 the ancient laws were renounced by Liholiho, Kamehameha II. The ancient gods were burned and the nation was free of their rule. With the overthrow of the gods went the religious rituals connected with the lei. Only the devout and the isolated still offered prayers and gifts to the gods and practiced the rites of the temple and the home.

The first Christian missionaries from New England arrived in 1820 on the brig Thaddeus. They were followed by several more companies through 1894. They brought many changes. They, along with other resident and transient haoles, white foreigners, influenced the lives and history of the Hawaiian people. The missionary women are credited with the introduction of various roses, violets, pansies, carnations, marigolds, and other American garden-type materials, which eventually were used by the Hawaiian lei maker.

The Chinese sailors, traders, farmers and contract laborers who settled in Hawai'i between 1823 and 1864 are credited for the introduction of such lei materials as pīkake *(Jasminum sambuc)*, pakalana *(Telosma cordata)*, mei sui lan, Chinese rice flower *(Aglaia ordorata)*, pua pākē *(Chrysanthemum morifolium, C. indicum)*, kiele *(Gardenia augusta)*, and pōpō-hau *(Hydrangea macrophylla)*. Like the early settlers of the Pacific, the Chinese, too, brought with them some treasure or momento of home to help them adjust to their new environment.

Dr. William Hillebrand lived in Hawai'i from 1851 to 1871 during which time he collected specimen and made notes for the first comprehensive book on Hawaiian flora. His book, Flora of the Hawaiian Islands, was published in 1888 two years after his death and serves as one of the principal resources for this writing on the leis of Hawai'i.

As Commissioner of Immigration to China and the East Indies from 1865 to 1866, Hillebrand collected plants and birds for introduction to Hawai'i. Some of his introductions soon became materials for the lei maker.

Other world travellers and immigrants collected materials and brought them to Hawai'i where they flourished and were soon used by the resourceful Hawaiian lei maker. Introduced materials became so much a part of Hawaiian life that soon many people forgot their origins and believed them to be native to the islands. Collectors introduced exotic plants from tropical America and the West Indies, Asia and the East Indies, Australia, New Zealand, the Pacific Islands and Africa. People who settled in the Islands' higher altitudes brought in temperate and alpine zone plants. Today, Hawai'i's flora is like Hawai'i's people—multi-racial and often cross-bred. The lei and customs associated with it took on this character of many races and intermixture.

Western man's influence became obvious in politics, religion, business, agriculture, domestic affairs, architecture and art. Whether this influence was all for the good of the Hawaiian is often disputed. Under this influence, the arts suffered much. The great wood sculpture was lost with the burning of the gods, even before art historians could make records of it. The loom woven fabrics of the Chinese, Europeans, and Americans replaced the fine bark cloth and the feather garments of the chiefs. Canoes gave way to Western sailing ships. The temples and thatched houses became New England churches and wood framed dwellings. All the handcrafted functionally beautiful implements designed for use in daily living were no longer made because there was no need for them. The twined baskets, the wooden calabashes, the decorated gourd containers were replaced by metal, ceramic, glass and wood vessels of the foreigners. Only the dance, the music, the lei endured the influences and capitalized upon them.

In the late 1800s Hawai'i's pleasant climate, wonderous scenery, and congenial people began to interest the adventuresome world travellers. The Hawaiian Hotel opened its doors to visitors and regular steamship service to the United States, Australia, New Zealand and points beyond was inaugurated. Visitors to the Sandwich Islands made special note of the fragrant and colorful garlands worn by the natives and some of the local haoles, which were sometimes presented to them on arrival.

Isabella Lucy Bird was one such visitor and in letters written between January and August, 1873, to her sister Henrietta of Edinburgh, she describes vividly the temporary leis of those times, the people who wore them, and the occasions on which they were worn.

She watched the abundant Princess Ruth Ke'elikolani board the Steamship Kilauea with immense leis of oleander about her head and shoulders. She wrote of King Lunalilo and his attendants at a reception in Hilo, . . . "almost concealed by wreaths of ohia blossoms and festoons of maile some almost two yards long, which had been thrown over them, and which bestowed a fantastic glamour on the otherwise prosaic inelegance of their European dress." Then she told of Lunalilo's subjects at the same reception wearing . . . "wreaths of Microlepia tenuifolia . . . All wore two, three, four or even six beautiful leis, besides festoons of the fragrant maile. Leis of crimson ohia blossoms were universal, but besides these there were leis of small red and white double roses, pohas, yellow amaranth, cane tassels like frosted silver, the orange pandanus, the delicious gardenia, and a very few orange blossoms, and the great grandilla or passion flower." She was greeted upon arriving at Hilo by glee singers who actually came to greet someone else, but who gave to her and other arriving passengers beautiful "garlands of roses and ohias." In this letter to her sister, she made note of this arrival with, " . . . music, flowers, goodwill and kindliness made us welcome to these enchanted shores." She described the horseback riders as always wearing leis as they galloped through the streets of Honolulu on evening rides or as they picked their way carefully down sides of steep valley walls. Soon she was wearing them as she rode astride Kahele, her horse, while she explored the island of Hawai'i.

The Kings and Queens of Hawai'i passed and another Hawaiian institution was lost to antiquity, but the lei remained, though changing, because of the addition of new materials, and an increase in the number of tourists who began to frequent "the loveliest fleet of islands anchored in any ocean."

By 1900 picturesque, lei-laden native men and women lined the piers at Honolulu's waterfront and for a few cents local residents could purchase chrysanthemum, carnation, 'ilima, rose, maile, pansy, violet, gardenia, and paper star leis to present to arriving friends, relatives, and business associates. A practice that had begun quite naturally a few years before and which had sprung from the even older custom of honoring loved ones and persons of rank, became a part of a budding tourist industry and things that are traditionally Hawaiian.

"For you a lei of flowers rare
For you a lei to hold and wear
For you a lei to caress when you go away
Throw your troubles away
And be happy and gay
A lei of love I give to you
To think of me when you are blue
Wherever you may be
Over land or over sea
For you a lei to remember me."[6]

The departures of visitors or relatives were like their arrivals, lei-laden. Soon someone threw a lei overboard, perhaps the flowers made him nauseous or gave him hay fever. He may have been truly saddened by his departure and hoping to return, cast his lei overboard as a gesture, a promise to come back. He may have been disgusted and disenchanted by Hawai'i, its people and its way of life and to show his disgust and disenchantment, he threw his leis overboard. Whatever the reason, the newly established Tourist Bureau latched on to the romantic probability; cast your lei overboard and the ocean currents will carry it back to shore, and that shall be your sign. You will return to Hawai'i someday.

Prominent Hawaiians scoffed at the promotion of such a fantasy. And with pen in hand, they wrote the editors of the newspapers to voice their objection to what was being labelled "a truly Hawaiian custom." They argued that the Hawaiian does not throw away a token of love. It is not in his tradition. The argument was filed away in the newspaper morgue and the perpetuators of "a truly Hawaiian custom" perpetuated it until it very soon gave way to air travel.

In 1923 the Territorial Legislature of Hawai'i passed a joint resolution designating certain natural materials as being the official emblem of each of the eight major islands and the territory. It is easy to understand the logic used in making the selection of the emblems for seven of the islands, but the choice of one of these, defies logic. All, but the lokelani or roselani, emblem for Maui, are native or had been brought to Hawai'i by early Polynesian settlers, and were mythically, poetically, and naturally associated with the island each represented prior to their official selection by the Legislature. All were for hundreds of years used as lei materials.

Hanohano Hawai'i moku o Keawe,
E lei ha'a heo nei i ka lehua.
Kilakila o Maui Haleakalā,
Ua kapu Roselani nāu ho'o kahi.
Kaulana Moloka'i nui a Hina,
I ka ulu kukui o Lanikaula.
Lei ana Lāna'i i ke kauna'oa.
Me he manu 'ō'ō hulu melemele.
Eia Mai au Kaho'olawe,
Ho'oheno ana au me ka hinahina.
Hea aku mākou ō mai 'oe;
Molokini 'alo ke 'ehu o ke kai.
Kaulana O'ahu i ka 'ilima,
Kohu kapa 'ahu'ula kau po'ohiwi.
Kaulana Kaua'i i ka mokihana,
Laua'e o Makana ka'u aloha.

[6] From a song, FOR YOU A LEI, by Johnny Noble and Oscar Hyatt. Johnny Noble's Royal Collection of Hawaiian Songs.

Pupu Ni'ihau auhea 'oe,
Hoike a'e 'oe a i ko nani.
Haina 'ia mai ana ka puana,
Nā lei o Hawai'i e ō mai.
Haina hou 'ia mai ana ka puana,
Hi'iaka ia kapoli a o Pele.[7]

Majestic Hawai'i home of Keawe,
Now proudly wearing garlands of lehua.
Surmounting regal Maui, Haleakalā
Reserv'd is roselani for you alone.
Renowned Moloka'i, great isle of Hina,
The kukui grove of Lanikaula.
The lei of Lānā'i, sweet kauna'oa,
Like the 'ō'ō bird's lovely yellow feathers.
Here I am waiting, Kaho'olawe,
Abounding are my shores in fragrant hinahina.
We call upon you, oh, give an answer,
Molokini endures the foam of the sea.
Famed is O'ahu for her 'ilima
Like a feather cape adorning the shoulders.
Famed is Kaua'i for mokihana,
Laua'e of Makana, garden of my home land.
Shells of Ni'ihau, where are you hiding?
O pearls of the sea show forth your beauty.
Now my story is thus completed—
O garlands of Hawai'i, awaken to our song.
And now I sing again, my song is over,
Hi'iaka of the sea, beloved Pele.

In 1928 Lei Day was established. At the suggestion of Don Blanding, an American poet who was overwhelmed by the visual and traditional beauty of the lei, the Bank of Hawai'i presented the first Lei Day Pageant with lei queen, island princesses, music, dance and lei contest on May 1 in Honolulu. Leis came from all the islands, wrapped in the customary pū'olo, tī leaf bundles or newspaper and cardboard boxes. School children, lei ladies and lei men, florists and ordinary everyday people competed for a grand prize of fifty dollars and various division prizes of twenty-five dollars.

"May Day is Lei Day in Hawai'i
Garlands of flowers ev'rywhere,
All of the colors in the rainbow
Maidens with blossoms in their hair
Flowers that mean we should be happy,
Throwing aside a load of care,
Oh, May Day is Lei Day in Hawai'i
Lei Day is happy day out there."[8]

Very few introduced materials, natural and man-made, escaped the lei maker's creative hands and aesthetic judgment. At one time or other since the arrival of the haole in Hawai'i, the lei maker has tried to use almost every introduced plant material. Some of these plant materials proved to be inappropriate for leis and never gained popularity, while others became so popular that present day Hawaiians label them "traditional."

Silk, satin, felt, and other fabrics; crepe paper, writing paper, cellophane, wood fibers, rick-rack, ribbons, yarn, and such mundane materials as cigarette wrappers, cordial bottles, candy, preserved fruits, U.S. currency and coins became raw materials for leis. The newest leis are made of molded plastic shapes which imitate the flowers, shells, and seeds of the traditional and contemporary leis of Hawai'i and most often are made in Hong Kong and Japan to fill especially the needs of the tourist industry and those who want "things" to last forever. A necessary evil, progress, a clever money-making idea, some say of the plastic flower leis, while others shudder and cry out, fake, phoney! Make plastic leis, but please, oh please, don't make plastic imitations.

[7] p. 17 Folk Songs Hawai'i Sings, John Kelly, Jr. Charles Tuttle Co., Inc., Japan. NA LEI O HAWAI'I also NA MOKU EWALU, the Reverend Samuel Kapu c. 1890

[8] From a song, MAY DAY IS LEI DAY IN HAWAI'I, by "Red Hawk" 1928. Songs of Hawai'i, Charles E. King, 1950, Honolulu.

Lei niho palaoa with spindle shape beads (top left); Wearing the Lei niho palaoa with spindle shape beads (top right); Pheasant Leis (center); Peacock Leis (bottom left); Wearing the Lei hulu manu (bottom right).

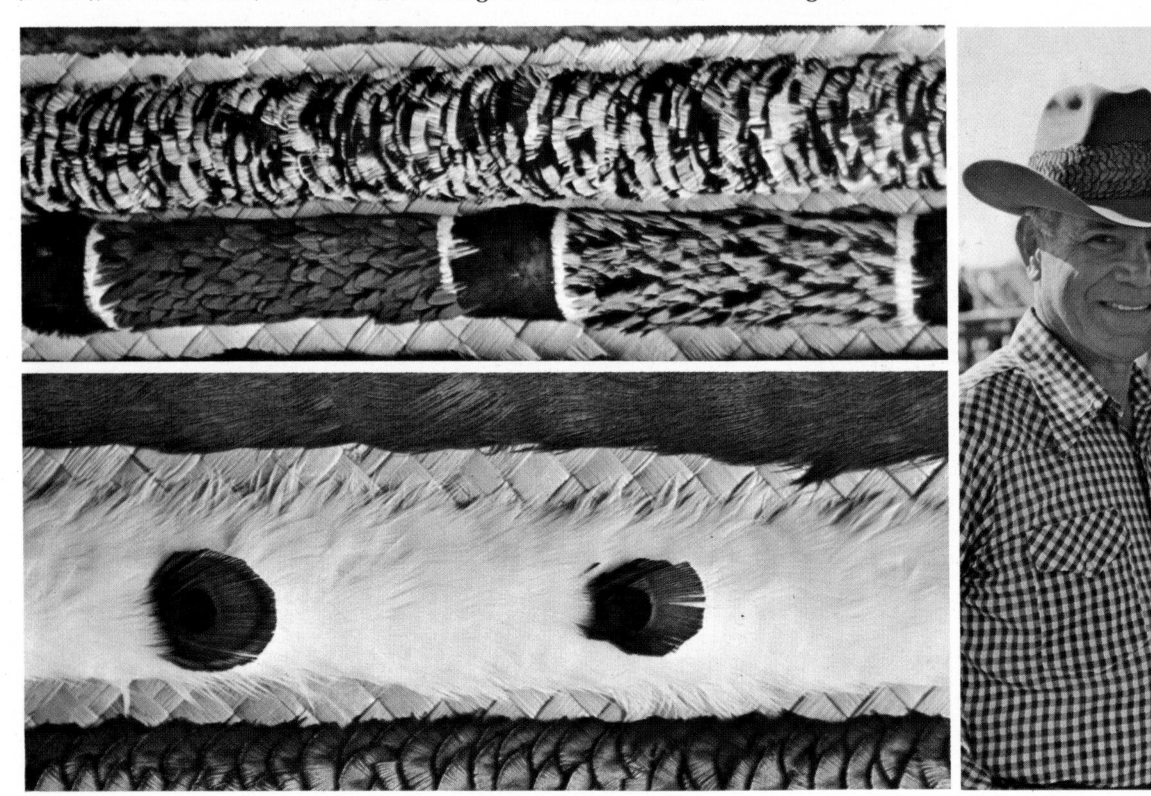

Wearing the Lei pūpū o Ni'ihau (left); Lei pūpū o Ni'ihau (right); Lei pūpū o Ni'ihau (bottom)

Some of the ancient permanent leis disappeared as times and needs changed. As Hawaiian royalty became more "westernized," the lei niho palaoa gives way to leis of pearls, diamonds, emeralds and other precious stones which are also the mark of all the other royalty the world over.

CONTEMPORARY IVORY, FEATHER AND SHELL LEIS

Fewer lei niho palaoa are seen as each year passes. Today some are seen on special Hawaiian holidays and on occasions when Hawaiians are honored, being worn by collectors or entertainers or descendants of ancient chiefs and chiefesses. Some contemporary craftsmen have made replicas of the ancient hook-shaped pendant but have never reproduced the suspension coils of human hair, perhaps because the eight strand square braid was too difficult to reproduce.

Another symbol of royalty, the lei hulu manu, disappears almost completely, since man and introduced birds and animals take over the forest in which native birds live. The lack of feathers from native birds, however, did not discourage the haku lei hulu manu (feather lei maker). Feathers from introduced birds were used, sometimes dyed with man-made colors. White chicken, duck, goose, and gooney bird feathers were dyed. Feathers from parrots, various kinds of pheasant, Guinea fowls, pea fowls, doves, quails, chickens, ducks, chukkers, francolins and other birds are used today with the Chinese ringneck pheasant and peacock feathers being the most desired. Although the ancient technique of attaching the feathers to a central cord with a binding thread is still used, the newer (when applied to feather leis) technique of sewing the feathers to a foundation of felt or flannel or other fabrics (humu-papa or kui papa) is more popular. The popularity of the humu-papa technique in feather lei making today is attributed to the introduction of the hat. Feathers are sewn to one side of the foundation. Each feather is attached with two or more overcast stitches. This kind of feather lei is called lei hulu papa, flat feather lei.

Island hunters will skin the birds, cure the skins with borax, salt or alum, and then sell them to lei makers. More often than not, these lei makers are wives of hunters. When enough skins are collected, the desired feathers are removed, sorted, and clipped if they are large. If they are the tiny feathers that usually come from the neck, they are not clipped. Feathers of like color, size, and shape, are kept together in covered paper, glass, wooden or plastic containers. A single feather is usually attached to the outside of the container so that the lei maker will know what kind of feathers are stored inside without opening the container. Preparation, that is, sorting and clipping, is time consuming.

The foundation is cut and folded to the desirable length and width of the lei, then stitched. Some lei makers add an extra piece of folded fabric a little narrower than the basic one by stitching it down the center of the original. The extra piece helps to give an otherwise flat lei, a curved fullness, which Hawaiians prefer and which they call hāpu'u or hāpu'upu'u. Expert feather lei makers say that the extra piece of folded fabric is not necessary. The pu'u, hill, forms naturally if the feathers are arranged and stitched in place properly, that is with quill ends and center of the feather pointing toward the center of the foundation at an angle, and not running parallel to the outside edges of the foundation. The middle feather of each row of feathers is stitched in place first with two, three, or four overcast stitches at various intervals in the lower three-quarters of the feather. A feather is added on either side of the middle one. The feathers are added alternately until the crescent shaped row is finished. Another crescent shaped row is added. The overlapping of feathers and stitches reinforces each preceding row. More rows are added until the lei is completed. Arranging the feathers in this fashion causes a build-up down the center of lei and the pu'u, hill, is formed naturally.

Each feather lei maker, as do makers of other kinds of leis, has her own special tricks which makes feather lei making easier for her. She may stretch her foundation fabric on a wide "u" shaped, wooden frame or she may attach it to the back of a straight back chair, or she may simply hold it in her hands. She may arrange her feathers running more or less parallel with the outside edge of her foundation. She may start by stitching her feathers from left to right, or right to left sides of her foundation or she may start by stitching sparsely spaced feathers along both edges, and for the entire length of the foundation. She may arrange her feathers closer together than some other lei maker may. She may stitch the feathers down with the concave curve facing toward (down) the foundation or she may stitch the feathers in place with the concave curve facing (up) away from the foundation or she may use a combination of the two curves.

One feather lei maker I know, sometimes makes bunches of feathers by tying several feathers together in a rossette, first. The bunches of rosettes are tied together as in a lei wili, then attached to a velvet ribbon and worn on a hat.

There has been little change in the lei pūpū since ancient times. Shells are still gathered, pierced, and strung on strands of fiber of some kind. Hawaiians today use fine drills or dental tools, or strong metal needles or fingernail clippers to make holes, and string the shells on monofilament or nylon thread. The finest lei pūpū still come from Ni'ihau where families who live there fill their free time shell collecting, sorting, and stringing the shells in various arrangements.

Contemporary Hawaiians have added some new techniques to shell lei making. (See illustration, plate 9 page 93). The first new technique (not new for fresh material lei making) was added at the turn of the century about the same time as the lei hulu papa. 'Ōlepe shells *(Chlamys loxoides)* which are sometimes called Hā'ena shells because they were found on the beach at Hā'ena, Kaua'i, were drilled and fastened to a foundation of cloth by sewing with a needle and thread. The white, sometimes spotted, sometimes pink ribbed bivalves were drilled with two holes through the area of the shell called umbo. The shells were arranged in equal lines of three or more, that is, if the first line had three valves, every line there after had three valves. Another arrangement was, every other line had the same number of valves. For example, if the first line had three valves, the second would have two, the third would have three, the fourth would have two and so on. Still another arrangement was to set the valves in slanted rows from side to side instead of straight across the width of the foundation. Each row would overlap the preceding one at least half way resembling fish scales. These lei pūpū are worn on hats and sometimes around heads.

'Kaulana no oe e nani Ni'ihau
Pupu lei nani o ka aina
He nani heihei oi kelakela
Ka lei a'i o kahelelani
No mai ko aloha pili me a'u
Ke aloha pumehana no Ni'ihau
E o e Ni'ihau i kou inoa
Pu'uwai 'olu'olu me ke aloha."[9]

You are famous oh beautiful Ni'ihau
For the beautiful shell lei of the land.
You are dignified and can boast
Of the neck lei of kahele-lani shells
Your love draws neigh to me
That warm love known only on Ni'ihau
Answer as we call your name, Ni'ihau
Your heart is full of kindness and love.

[9] From a song, NI'IHAU, by Kai Davis.

Another new technique used in shell lei making is a variation in stringing which present day Hawaiians call, pīkake, because finished leis resemble jasmine leis especially if the shells are small and white. Two long lengths of nylon thread are divided in half and slip knotted at the center. The slip knot is anchored to a nail or staple on a board or table. The four thread ends are burned to melt the fibers or they are tipped off with quick drying glue to make a hard point which is used in place of a needle. Tiny pūpū Ni'ihau *(Euplica varians)* are prepared by snipping off the spire tips (if they have not been worn down by water and sand action) with fingernail clippers and tapping out a hole through the body whorl opposite the aperture with an awl. Working with two strings on one side of the slip knot, the first shell is strung spire end first on one string, while the second shell is strung on the other string. The two strings are square knotted together. The stringing continues, one shell on each string, knot and so on until half of the lei is completed, then the slip knot at the center is removed and the lei is anchored at the end of the first half. The stringing for the second half is the same as the stringing of the first half resulting in the shells of the first half and the shells of the second half meeting at the center front of the lei with spires touching and at center back of the lei with apertures facing each other. The lei is usually finished with a clasp of a cowry shell.

Straight stringing is called kui pololei, stringing true. Round stringing or stringing as a rope is called kui poepoe. Stringing with shells alternating from side to side is called kui lau, stringing in a leaf design. (See illustration, plate 9 page 93).

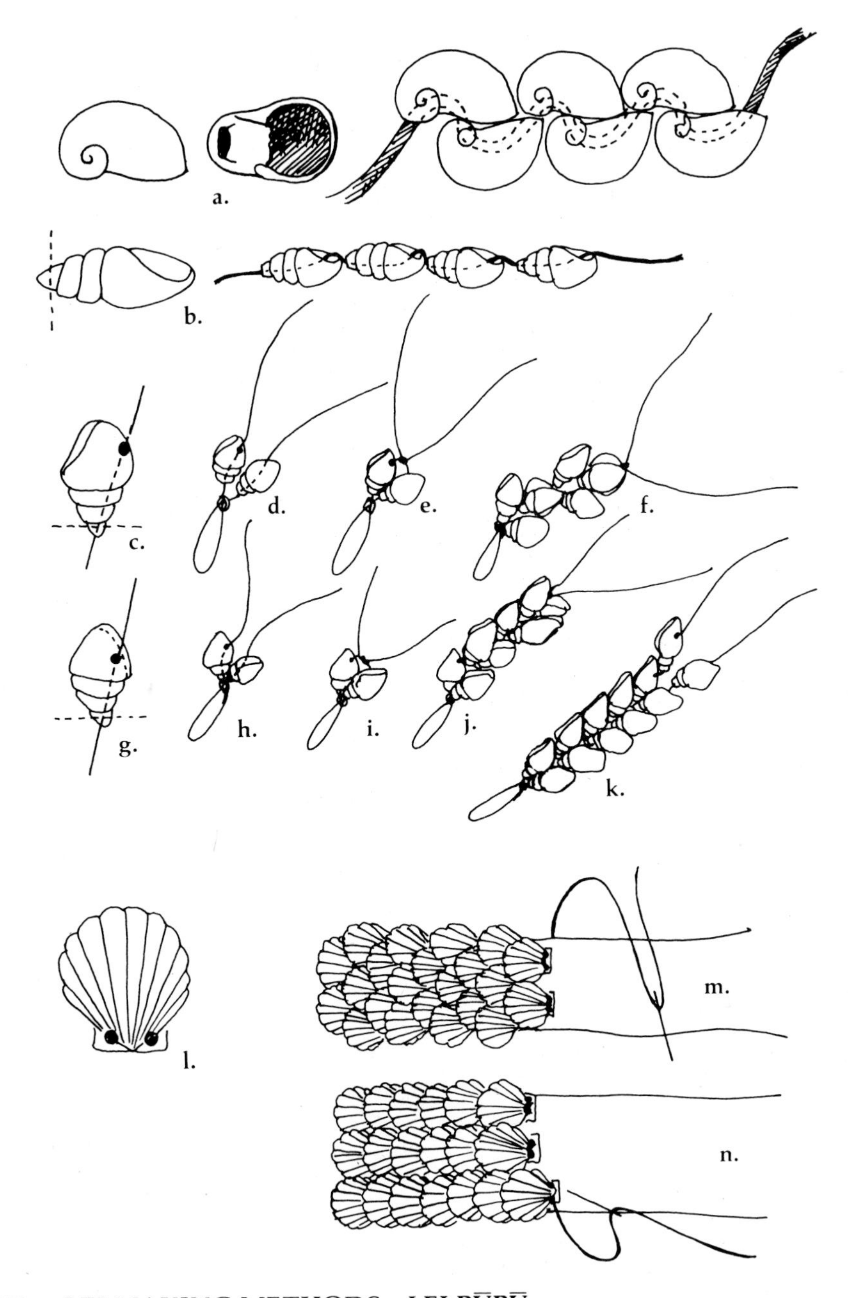

PLATE 9. LEI MAKING METHODS—LEI PŪPŪ

a. lei kupeʻe
b. pūpū o Niʻihau—lei pololei
c. position of punched out hole for kui lau and kui pīkake
d. shells are strung on two strings, knotted together with an overhand knot after each set of two shells for lei lau, and
e. a square knot after each set of two shells for lei pīkake
f. the pattern is repeated for lei pīkake
g. position of punched out hole for kui poepoe
h. stringing shells
i. square knotting strings after each set of two shells
j. the pattern is repeated for lei poepoe
k. lei lau
l. position of holes in ʻōlepe shell for kui papa
m, n. arrangements of shells for lei papa

Lei ōlepe (top). Puka shell and paper shell leis (bottom).

Seed Leis. False wiliwili, Job's tears, canna and ēkoa (top left). Se Leis. Pili nut, tamarind, black walnut, skunk tree, Madagascar oli and canna (top right). Lei 'ōlepe (bottom).

Kākalaioa seed lei (top left), Loulu seed leis (top right), Lei pūpū kuahiwi (bottom).

Wearing the Lei hua

SHELLS USED IN LEI MAKING BY NI'IHAU NATIVES

"Pūpū" is the general name for all shells. It is usually followed by one or more specific, descriptive names. Example: "pūpū momi ke'oke'o, white, pearl shell. For proper Hawaiian classification all names must be used. However, shells are listed below by specific, descriptive name only. They are listed first, by their Ni'ihau name, then their other names, i.e. names as given in the Hawaiian Dictionary by Pukui and Elbert in parenthesis, and finally by their scientific names. Remarks will follow each listing. These are the most commonly used shells.

1. Kāmoa, ('ālīlea), *Turbo sandwicensis*

   The very young, small turbos are used in leis or the larger ones are cut down with fingernail cutters until only the yellow tip of the spire is left. These spire tips are strung through a hole that is punched out through the top. Leis of only these spire tips are rare and unbelievable. Usually pūpū kāmoa is used to add interest to leis of other shells. The spire tips resemble the yellow spores of the primitive plant called moa *(Psilotum nudum)*, thus the name, kāmoa.

   The most commonly used shell for leis from Ni'ihau are from the family Columbellidae, *Euplica varians*. These shells range in color from white through brown.

2. Momi ke'oke'o maika'i, momi ke'oke'o, momi maika'i, (pūpū-Ni'ihau), *Euplica varians*

   These small shells are pure white.

3. Momi uli uli, uli uli, (pūpū-Ni'ihau), *Euplica varians*

   Shells are the same as above in size and shape. They are different in color. These are tinged with blue.

4. Momi kahakaha, kahakaha, (pūpū-Ni'ihau), *Euplica varians*

   Shells are the same as above in size and shape. They are different in color and markings. These are brown striped.

5. 'Ōnikiniki, 'ula'ula, momi 'ōnikiniki 'ula'ula, (pūpū-Ni'ihau), *Euplica varians*

   Shells are the same as above in size and shape. They are different in color and markings. These are brown spotted overall.

6. Kua 'ula'ula, momi kua 'ulu'ulu (pūpū-Ni'ihau), *Euplica varians*

   Shells are the same as above in size and shape. They are different in color and markings. These are brown spotted on the back and at the canal.

   NOTE: There are some Ni'ihau people who call all Euplica varians, *momi o kai, pearl of the sea, without noting their subtle differences. These are the most commonly used shells for Ni'ihau leis.*

7. 'Ālīlea, (pūpū-mamāiki), *Strombus maculatus*

   'Ālīlea is the name Pukui and Elbert give for *Turbo sandwicensis*.

8. Lā'iki, laiki, *Mitrella margarita*

   When compared with *Euplica varians*, these shells are narrower, thus the name la'iki, slim or narrow, however, some sources prefer laiki, since the shells do resemble grains of rice. They are small, white and sometimes marked with a few brown spots. They are very popular for leis.

9. Lōloa, *Mitrella zebra*

10. Mauna Loa, (pūpū-lei-'aha'aha), *Mitra litterata*

11. Kauno'o, *Heliacus variegatus*

    This shell is commonly called the variegated sundial. The Hawaiian name means scorched, partly consumed by fire, inflamed. It is often used at the ends of several strands of shells. The thread ends of several strands are drawn through a hole that is punched out of the spire tip of the shell before they are finally secured in a cowry shell clasp.

12. Kahele-lani, *Leptothyra verruca*

    These tiny brown, tan red, and pink shells are the most valuable of the Ni'ihau shells. The Hawaiian name means the royal going. Some say that these shells were so called because they were worn by members of the ali'i class.

13. 'Awa, pāpale pākē, *Trochus historio*

    Pūpū 'awa, according to Pukui and Elbert, is the name for other shells, *Drupa ricinus, Thais aperta.* The name means, sour, bitter, or poisonous. Pāpale pākē is a more recent name meaning Chinese hat.

    A number of cowries are used by the Ni'ihau lei maker. Most often they are used for the clasps on the necklaces. Sometimes they are strung up into leis with the thread being held in place through their apertures with a stuffing of cotton and glue. According to Pukui and Elbert, leho is the general name for cowry shell. On Ni'ihau pōleho or pōleholeho is a small sized cowry. Pōleho is also used to indicate a dark or burnt color.

14. Pōleholeho 'ōpu'upu'u, pōleholeho ke'oke'o, (leho 'ōkala), *Cypraea granulata*

    This cowry is endemic to the Hawaiian Islands.

15. Pōleholeho 'ōnikiniki, pōleholeho 'ele'ele, (leho kupa), *Cypraea caputserpentis*
16. Pōleholeho lenalena, (leho kupe'e lima), *Cypraea isabella*
17. *Cypraea tessellata* is also called poleholeho lenalena because of its yellowish brown color. *C. tessellata* is endemic to Hawai'i.
18. Pōlehō māku'e, (leho 'opule) *Cypraea helvola*
19. Lenalena, *Pinaxia versicolor*
20. 'Ōlepe, ('olepe), *Chlamys loxoides*

    This is a bi-valve of which the upper half is brown and white and the lower half is pure white. It is endemic to the Hawaiian Islands. The valves are pierced and sewn to a foundation or they are pierced in the center and strung on cord.[10]

The leis of beach worn disks of the cone *(Conus)* shells are enjoying a re-birth today under the name of "puka shell necklace." A lei of tiny, matched white disks is more valuable than leis of larger, white, lavendar or brown disks. Islanders spend many hours sifting sand for the worn disks. The disks are strung through naturally worn holes in their centers or holes are stamped out or drilled.

Newest of the present day shell leis are called "paper shell necklaces." The "paper shells" come from shell (test) bearing protozoa that are found in shallow water around the islands. When the one-celled animals die, their "shells" of siliceous or calcareous material drop to the bottom of the sea and are later washed up on the shore where they become a part of the sand. The sand is sifted for these tiny, paper thin, irregular disks. Holes are punched through the middle of the disks with a needle or a dental or pointed metal tool for stringing. Shells are from the protozoan *Sarcodina foraminifera.* The shells are shades of white, pink and brown and are an eighth of an inch in diameter. The lei pūpū pepa is delicate and needs to be handled with care.

CONTEMPORARY SEED LEIS

More lei hua or lei'ano'ano seed necklaces, were made as new plants with tough shelled seeds were introduced and became common. The steel tipped drill and especially the electric drill has made seed lei making a popular pastime. Many seeds are simply drilled and strung straight, kui pololei or in various patterns, while others must have dull, sometimes fibrous, outer layers removed by a tedious process of filing, sanding and finally polishing with buffing compounds and jeweler's rouge. Contemporary craftsmen have invented special jigs for holding the seeds securely in place for drilling and polishing.

Many hours are required for the polishing of some nuts. The kukui nut which was and is still the most popular nut for the lei hua is still difficult to polish. Although some nuts are polished by using mechanical devices throughout, the finest lei kukui still consists

[10] List prepared with the help of Betsy Harrison Gagne, and John and Annette Ka'ohelauli'i.

of nuts that are hand polished.

The kukui nut is not smooth. It is irregularly grooved much like the ordinary English walnut. Jeweler's flat, triangular, and round files are used to get into the grooves to remove the white, lime-like deposits that cover the nut. Sanding with wet-dry sand paper of various grits follows. The process is tedious even with modern day tools. Then each nut is drilled with one hole and attached to a metal pin. The pin is inserted into the chuck of a quarter or half horsepower motor and polished with jeweler's rouge and a soft cloth. Another method is: several nuts are drilled through and are strung on wire after the filing and sanding is completed. The ends of the wire are tied together. The craftsman holds onto the circle of nuts for polishing on a buffing wheel.

Removing the nut meats is still a chore. There are craftsmen who pick out the meats through the tiny drilled openings. There are those who leave the nuts laying around in a protected place for insects to eat out the nut meats through the tiny openings or they wait for the natural process of decay to work. Some craftsmen use a solvent to eat away the nut meat. The solvent makes the nut shell darker which is what many people like.

Some seeds need not be drilled. The pū'ohe'ohe or Job's tears *(Coix lachryma-jobi)* have natural openings through their centers. The ēkoa *(Leucaena leucocephala)* seeds are boiled until soft then pierced with a needle. Boiled seeds can be kept in a tightly closed container for several days. Ēkoa seeds and Job's tears seeds are strung into many different patterns, some very simple and others very ornate. Sometimes the seeds are used together or combined with other seeds. (See illustration, plate 10 page 99).

Other commonly used seeds which need not be polished are false wiliwili *(Adenanthera pavonina)*; pūkiawe-lei, black-eyed Susan or bead vine, *(Abrus precatorius)*; 'opiuma, Manila tamarind, *(Pithecellobium dulce)*; mānele, a'e or soapberry, *(Sapindus saponaria)*; kā'e'e or sea bean, (*Mucuna urens* and *M. gigantea)*; Kākalaioa, grey nickers, *(Caesalpinia major)*; elephant's ear *(Enterolobium cyclocarpum)*; 'ōhai or monkey pod *(Samanea saman)*; kolī, castor bean *(Ricinus communis)*; wiliwili *(Erythrina sandwicensis)*; mauna-loa *(Canavalia cathartica)*; wiliwili-haole *(Erythrina variegata)*; pua kelekino or Mysore thorn *(Caesalpinia sepiaria)*; 'ōhai-'ula, royal poinciana *(Delonix regia)*; and li'ipoe *(Canna indica)*.

Seeds or nuts which need to be husked, filed, sanded and polished are usually the palms. The most commonly used palms are the monkey nut, queen palm or feathery coconut palm *(Arecastrum romanzoffianum)*; the Manila palm, *(Veitchia merrillii)*; and the coconut *(Cocos nucifera)*. The shell of the coconut is cut into pieces of various shapes and sizes, polished, holes drilled in them, then linked together with metal loops, or strong cord or ribbon. Sometimes a single piece of coconut shell is used for a pendant.

Since the monkey nut and the Manila palm nut range in sizes of about one-half to one-inch in length, they are used whole. Often these nuts are combined with other seeds in interesting leis. One contemporary craftsman has combined monkey nuts with sperm whale ivory in a very handsome lei.

Other palm nuts which are used for leis are the latan palms *(Latania spp.)*; the oil palm *(Elaeis guineensis)*; cohune nut palm (*Orbigyna cohune)*; the loulu palm *(Pritchardia spp.)*; and the gru-gru palm *(Acrocomia ierensis)*.

Unusual leis are made with the split seed cases of the sandbox tree *(Hura crepitans)* or the odd shaped seeds of the chaulmoogra tree *(Hydnocarpus kurzii)*, or the beach worn nuts of the hala *(Pandanus odoratissimus)*.

Other seeds are used for leis. They are the seeds of the pili nut or Java almond *(Canarium vulgare)*; the akee *(Blighia sapida)*; the kamani *(Calophyllum inophyllum)*; woodrose *(Operculina tuberosa)*; blue marble tree *(Elaeocarpus grandis)*; the Java olive *(Sterculia foetida)*; black walnut

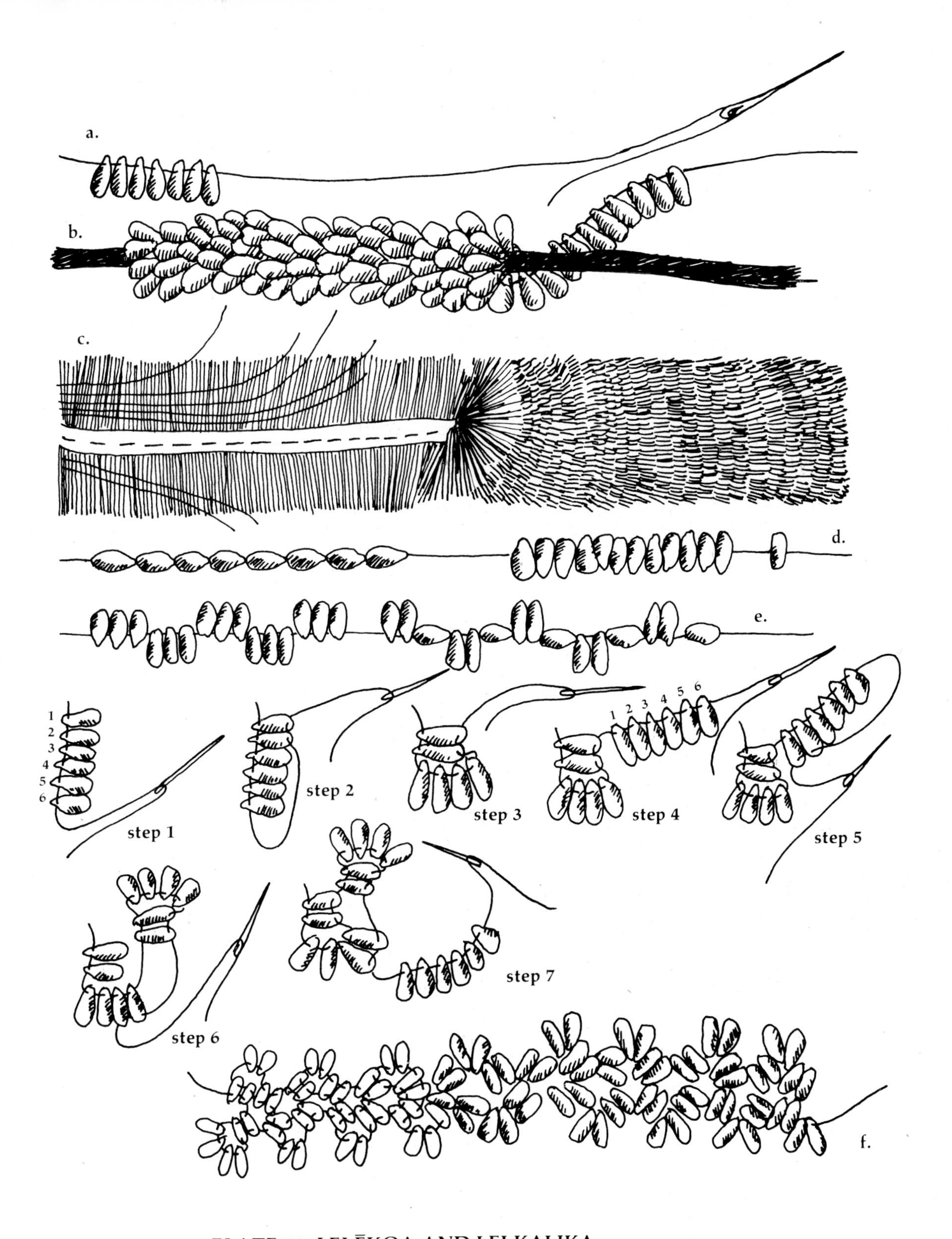

PLATE 10. LEI ĒKOA AND LEI KALIKA.

a. simple stringing of ēkoa seeds
b. wrapping strung seeds around a central cord
c. lei kalika: removing threads, stitching, and twisting
d. ēkoa: kui pololei—lengthwise and crosswise
e. ēkoa: varied stringing
f. ēkoa: flat stringing creating an ornate pattern

Silk and rick-rack leis (top), Paper Leis (center), Plastic Leis (bottom)

(Juglans nigra).

As the yellow and red feathers from native birds became scarce, Hawaiians substituted other materials. Yellow and red feathers of introduced birds were rare also, so that lei makers turned to either dyeing white feathers or finding another material which would mimic the lei hulu manu of ancient times. Strips of silk and later satin became the substitute material.

LEI KALIKA
(Silk Lei)

The lei kalika, or lei kilika, is made by first cutting strips of fabric, crosswise of the goods in widths of one to three inches (narrower or wider if preferred). Several strips are needed for one lei. Each strip is stitched with small running stitches down the center and passed onto a strong center thread of about fifty inches in length. The weft threads are removed from the outside edges of each strip of fabric to within an eighth of an inch of the center thread (running stitches). A needle or pin is often used for removing the weft threads. This step may be done in reverse. (See illustration, plate 10, page 99).

One end of the center thread is tied to the back of a straight back chair, a door knob, or a handy post, while the other end of that thread and the end of the first strip of fabric is held securely by the lei maker or attached to another door, etc. Each strip of silk is twisted a little at a time into full circle spirals, then pushed against the lei maker's holding fingers. The lei maker must take care in keeping the center thread taut while twisting and pushing. Twisting and pushing continues until all the strips are used up, then the lei is trimmed if needed.

LEI PEPA AND LEI 'EA
(Paper And Plastic Leis)

In later years, other fabric and crepe paper leis were made in the same way.

The paper lei, lei pepa, was probably an invention that grew out of the early tourist trade. Strips of crepe paper are sewn down the center or along one edge with short running stitches. Several strips cut crosswise from folds of crepe paper are needed to make one lei. The sewn strips are twisted into spirals and are pushed together tightly at one end of the thread. Sewing, twisting, and pushing together tightly continues until the lei is finished.

In the 1920s and 1930s the crepe paper lei makers invented some very ornate paper leis. The strips of crepe paper folds were cut along one or both edges with slits that were individually twisted; scallops that were left intact or wrinkled; alternating slits and scallops; rounded scallops; pointed scallops; and various combinations of slits and scallops. Sometimes two strips of different widths and color are stitched together for another effect. The finished leis resemble leis of 'ilima, poni mō'ī, 'awapuhi, and lehua (See illustration, plate 11, page 109).

THE LEI IN CONTEMPORARY DANCE, MUSIC, POETRY AND LORE

Paper leis are used at massive luaus and conventions. They are often slipped into gift packages of pineapples, macadamia nuts, hula skirts, 'ukuleles, jams, jellies, Kona coffee and other products of Hawai'i. The plastic lei, lei 'ea is replacing the paper lei at the lū'aus and conventions, and in the gift packages. These perfect visual replicas are often worn by the Hawaiian and Polynesian dancers of today.

It was about three in the afternoon. The telephone on my desk rang. I answered, "Ala Wai Clu . . ." before I could finish, the voice on the other end said, "hey, Gallahad." It was my father. He had called me Gallahad since the day of my first haircut which was when I was four or five years old. It seems I had had some problems growing hair. "Will you pick me up at the Kaimuki Inn on your way home," he asked. "Okay," I

Leis for Kamehameha

. . . at a wedding

. . . for a memorial

. . . for entertainers (top left)
. . . at the cemetery (top right)
. . . at graduation (left)

. . . for the pāʻū riders (top right)
. . . at a party (right)

. . . for the paniolo (top)
. . . to adorn a hat (bottom)

. . . Leis for the dancers (right)
. . . for young people (bottom left)
. . . for the older person (bottom right)

... for money (left)
... for children in pageantry (bottom left)
... for a Maui girl (bottom right)

answered, "that'll be about five o'clock, okay?" "Fine, fine." "Don't drink too many beers." "And now you are my mother?" "Oh, Daddy."

I parked my car, got out of it and entered the restaurant-bar. I saw Daddy immediately. He was sitting with a very hairy man—silver-grey, curly, hairy man. He had hair all over the top of his head and covering most of his face. It billowed out over the top of his body. He was neat looking. He wore a blue palaka shirt and faded blue jeans. "Hey, Gallahad," Daddy called to me as I walked towards him, "come meet my old friend Sheep." I did a double take, you know, a look and then another quick look. This guy really looked like a sheep. Dad was up to his old tricks of giving people descriptive names, I thought. The man stood as I came up to the table and said with an outstretched hand, "the name is Hīpā and it is sheep in Hawaiian and Spike (my father) is never going to use Hīpā. He has called me Sheep ever since your mother translated my name into English for him. Come on, sit down and have a beer." I sat, ate the pupus and listened to these two old guys. Sheep had been educated at some Mainland college and his English was flawless. He had just returned to the islands after several years of travelling and working abroad. He was telling us how things had changed when the subject turned to hula girls and as beautifully as he spoke "standard" English, Sheep slipped into pidgin.

"Eh, da hula girls nowadays, dey pretty good lookin', kina wīwī doe and dey no move like befo time. Dey wayah some long leis, down to da flowa almost. Wen dey hula onay da hands move like dey wen like hole one cup tea, da pinky stay up. Dey no move da 'okole and da waewae. If dey move um, broke 'ia the some long lei and maybe some ting moa and dey come some hilahila. Wen I ax dem, 'eh, how come you hula la dat?' Dey tell in high class talk, 'this is how it is done in these modern times, tūtū.' Ho, dey call me 'tūtū,' man I burn up. Dey tink I ole or what? But you wait, bum by all da kumu hula going tell, I like onay da momona wahines, jel like befo time and dose skinny buggas goin cry. I read in da pepa now dey goin get one renaissance of da ole kine stuff. As some beeg word, but I fine um in dat dictionary. One rebirt, rewhywall, da dictionary tell. Man, fo shoowa dose skinny buggas goin cry. Auwē nō ho'i ē!

The lei and its association with the hula and the music of Hawai'i continues. The hula is incomplete without it. In the late 1800's critics complained because the dancers of those times wore too many leis. Today, critics complain of dancers who wear leis down to their knees and even ankles. Too theatrical and too Hollywood.

During the last half of the 19th century, composers, such as, Lili'u-o-ka-lani, Lele-iō-Hōkū, Ka-lā-kaua, Likelike, and others tell of the beauties of the lei, and associate it with love of sweetheart, love of land, love of child, love of beauty. Their successors of the twentieth century, King, Ae'a Ke-alaka'i, Alohikea, Nape, Elia, Ka-lama, Huelani, Kāne, Holt, Beamer, Mossman, Noble, Almeida, and others continue the tradition through the next fifty years. Some contemporary song writers, Pukui, Namakelua, and Wong, echo the lyrical style of the writers of fifty or more years ago, while others, knowing now the language, use English words, which, though beautiful, lack the poetry and kaona, veiled language, of the Hawaiian lyrics.

"Ohaoha wale ku'u lei
I ka lihau ia e ka ua noe
Ka hikina ana mai o la po nei
Ho'o pumehana i ku'u poli."[11]

Ah, how precious is my wreath so charming
Jewelled with dewdrops of the forest
T'was last night I heard you swiftly coming
On your bosom warm I sank to rest.

[11] From a song, LEI OHAOHA, by Princess Likelike. Johnny Noble's Royal Collection of Hawaiian Songs, P. 112.

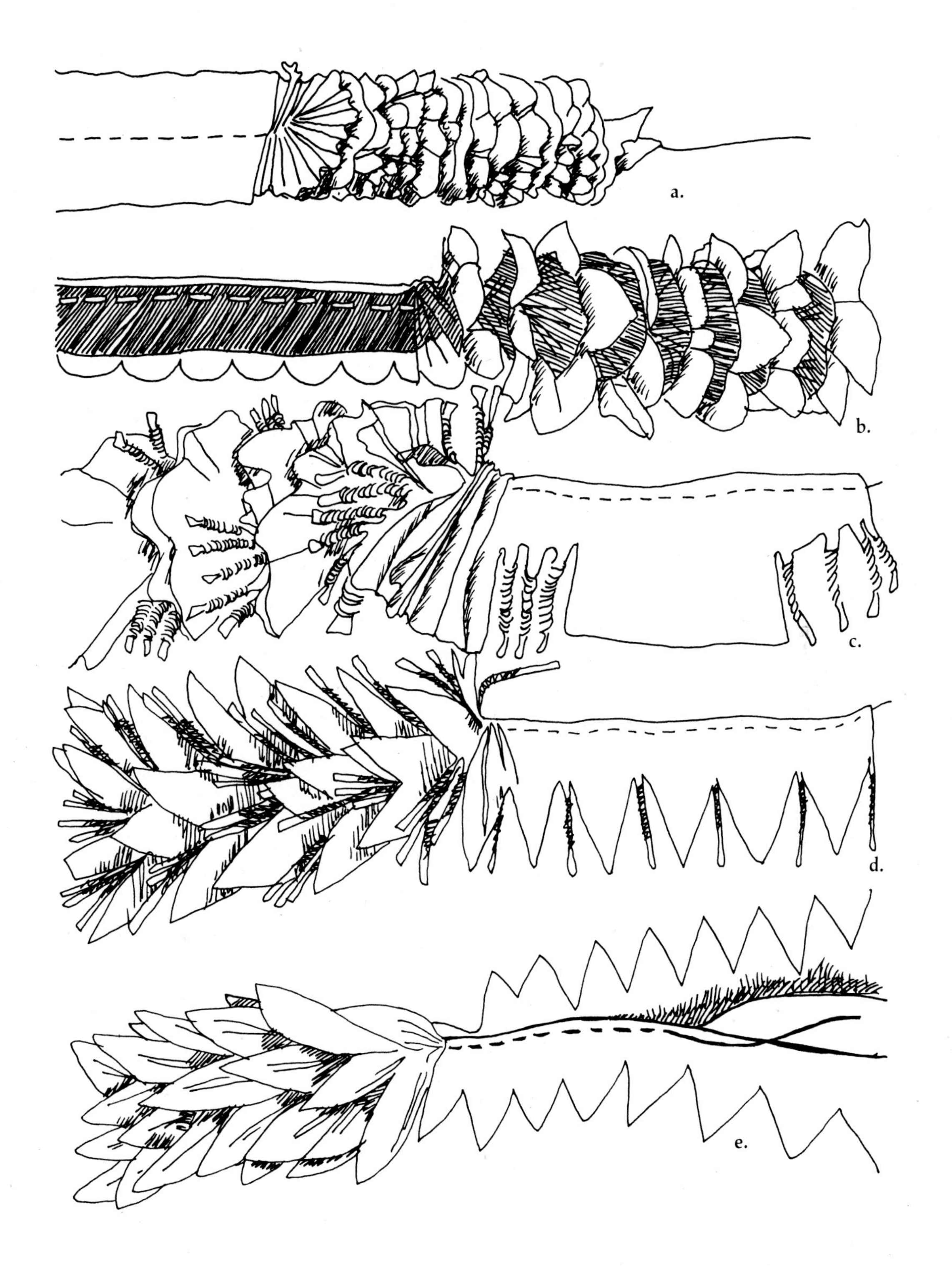

PLATE 11. LEI PEPA.

a. a single strip of crepe paper stitched down the center and twisted
b. two strips of different colored paper stitched together along one edge and twisted
c. a single strip of paper with cut and twisted design stitched along one edge and twisted
d. another cut and twisted design
e. two strips of paper with cut design, overlapping at the center stitched and twisted

"E ku'u lei, E ku'u lei
Lei aloha na'u
Lei makamae." [12]

My lei (my darling), my lovely one
Beloved one of mine
My precious one.

"Mama don't scold me, I no go work today
Down there in Iwilei, In the pineapple
cannery.
Mama don't scold me, I bring a lei for you
I sing all day for you, the songs of
Hawai'i."[13]
"You were wearing a blue lei
The day that I first met you
As we wandered by on the sand
Of the blue, blue sea . . . ."[14]

Those who sing the songs of Hawai'i, like those who dance to the songs of Hawai'i, still wear the leis of Hawai'i to enhance their song.

Traces of the once pagan Hawaiian custom of offering gifts, particularly leis to the gods, can be seen in Christian houses of worships and at Christian ceremonies today. Catholics decorate statues of patron saints with garlands of flowers. Protestants string ropes of flowers across the altars and pulpits. Leaders of Christian faiths consecrate and dedicate buildings with prayers and the untying of flower leis. In the religious ceremony of marriage, the pews and participants are marked with leis.

Today one sees the lei as often as in former years. Shell leis, feather leis, and seed leis are worn by all kinds of people as they go about the daily business of working, living, worshiping, and playing. Leis of fresh temporary materials appear at festivals, night clubs, luaus, weddings, graduations, dedications, dates, proms, athletic events, political campaigns, airport and oceanside farewells and hellos, in church, at retirement parties, at awards' banquets, at lectures on guest lecturers, on birthdays, at parades, draped over pictures, and at grave sites.

And so, an art form born in some distant past and out of man's emotional and aesthetic need to react and interact with his natural surroundings, to love and honor his fellow, and to adorn himself, evolves and survives the millenia of time.

[12]LEI ALOHA by Charles E. King. King's Book of Hawaiian Melodies, 1948, p. 144.
[13]From a song, FISH AND POI, anonymous. Probably put together by many people—each person adds a verse.
[14]BLUE LEI, Milton D. Beamer and R. Alex Anderson.

HĒ'Ī, MĪKANA, MILIKANA, PAPAIA, PAPAYA, PAWPAW, CARICA PAPAYA

A native of tropical America, the papaya was an early arrival in Hawai'i. It may have arrived in Hawai'i via Asia before the white man or at the latest, with or shortly after his arrival. Early travellers to the islands recorded it as being well established.

The papaya is noted for its edible fruit rather than its leis which are made from the small, fragrant, tubular, cream colored, male flowers. The fragrant flowers are reminiscent of the 'ōhā-wai blossoms which have long been used for leis. In recent years, the lei hē'ī has given way to other leis constructed of more flamboyant and more easily obtained materials. This rarely seen lei is made by stringing the blossoms lengthwise through their tubes, or by stringing the blossoms laterally through their tubes arranging them as spokes in a wheel.

"Aloha no paha 'oe
E ka pua o ka hē'ī
Ke i a'e no wau
O ka 'oi o Ka Pālama
Malama 'ia ko kino
O lilo mai ia nei
Ia nei no māua
I ka malu o ke kukui."[15]

"Greetings to you
O papaya flower
I say
It's the best of Pālama
Be careful of your body
Or it'll be lost
To the two of us
Under the shade of the kukui."

MAMO, SAFFLOWER, FALSE SAFFRON, CARTHAMUS TINCTORIUS

This native of Asia was introduced early in the Nineteenth Century. Marin reported planting the seeds in 1817. It was introduced and planted for economic reasons since the flowers produced a very popular yellow and red dye for cloth and rouge, and the seeds yielded oil for food, paint and varnish. Soon after Marin's planting, the safflower began to appear in many gardens. Hawaiians gave it the name "mamo" because the blossom's yellow-orange petals resembled the golden yellow tufts of mamo (*Drepanis pacifica*) feathers. The calyxes are split and the blossoms pierced (kui) lengthwise through their centers and strung on strong thread to produce the lei mamo or attached with ferns to a center cord with a binding thread.

Soon the lei mamo, like other leis of the times, became allied with love, lovers, and love-making as shown by the following lines from two songs composed during the late 1800s.

"Sweet lei mamo
Lei o ke aloha
Kāhiko nani o'u
Sweet lei mamo."[16]

Sweet lei mamo
Lei of love
My beautiful adornment,
Sweet lei mamo.

"A he lei mamo 'oe no ke ahiahi
E 'uhene ai me Li'a i ka uka."

"You are evening's lei of saffron flowers
Exalting with Li'a in the forest."[17]

HALA-KAHIKI, PINEAPPLE, ANANAS COMOSUS

Although some Hawaiians believe that the hala-kahiki was grown in Hawai'i before the arrival of Captain Cook, scientists generally agree that it was introduced sometime between Cook's arrival and 1813 when Don

[15] From a song, PUA O KA HE'I, by Eliza Holt, C. 1899—Johnny Noble's Royal Collection of Hawaiian Songs.

[16] From a song, "SWEET LEI MAMO," by Huelani. P. 92 Nā Mele O Hawai'i, Elbert and Mahoe.

[17] From a song, "HO'OHENO," by Jack Heleluhe and Joseph K. Ae'a. P. 54 Nā Mele O Hawai'i, Elbert and Mahoe.

Photos at left: Male papaya flowers (top)
Lei mīkana (second photo)
Mamo flowers (third photo)
Lei hala-kahiki (bottom)

Lei lokelani *(Rosa damascena)* (top right)
Damask rose (bottom right)

Lei lokelani *(Rosa chinensis)* (top left), Lei lokelani with mei sui lan (center left), China rose (bottom left), Wearing the Lei lokelani (above)

Marin recorded its presence in his garden. Pineapples were soon seen growing wild in Kailua, Kona where they got the name Wild Kailua. Hawaiians called the white tinged fruits hala-kea, and the red tinged one, hala-'ula.

Leis were made by cutting out the hexagonal sections of the shell, allowing them to dry out a little and stringing them on strong thread or stitching them to a foundation. The lei hala-kahiki has a pleasing scent which is why Hawaiians of the 1800s chose to wear it.

LOKELANI, ROSELANI, ROSA DAMASCENA, ROSA CHINENSIS 'LUIS FILIPE'

Two roses, neither native to Hawai'i, through the years, have been called lokelani, heavenly rose, by the Hawaiians who were fascinated by the color and scent of the blossoms.

Rosa damascena, the pink Damask rose, a native of Asia Minor was brought to the New World by the Spanish and introduced to Hawai'i in the early 1800s. Some say that seamen from New England introduced this rose which is sometimes called loke-Hawai'i. Others believe that the missionary women brought it with them. It may have been the rose which was used in a wreath for the lace cap that complemented the first holoku (a loose seamed dress with more or less of a train) worn by Kalakua (a wife of Kamehameha I) in 1820. Later, in 1829, C.S. Stewart reported it growing in the garden of Don Francisco Marin.

Soon the *Rosa damascena* became a very sought-after plant for Hawaiian gardens. It became so popular in the gardens of Lahaina, Maui that people finally nicknamed it the Maui rose. It was along the roses that grew at McKee's Ulupalakua Rose Ranch. Before long the poets and song composers began to sing its praises and they added the final touch by making the pink Damask rose synonymous with the Island of Maui. The Territorial Legislature of 1923 in a joint resolution, officially established the lokelani as the flower of Maui. It is the only post discovery plant to be recognized as the official flower of any of the Hawaiian Islands.

It is easy to understand why Hawaiians of the 1800's were fascinated by the Damask rose. It was beautiful to behold, sweetly scented, and when gathered in bud was most appropriate in a lei, as it stayed fresh and intact for a good length of time.

The Damask rose for some reason became very rare and soon the Hawaiians substituted another rose to take its place. They selected the *Rosa chinensis* 'Luis Filipe' probably because it was a hardy plant. Certainly they didn't choose it because it was pink and highly scented like the Damask rose—it wasn't—or because it lasted well as a cut flower and would hold up well in a lei—it didn't. They probably chose it because it was readily available and could survive the tropics and the pests that usually attack roses.

The *Rosa chinensis* 'Luis Filipe' probably was introduced by the Chinese. It is a small dark pink or red rose with a pink center. As a cut flower it does not last as well as other roses as it quickly falls apart. It is commonly used in hedges.

The lokelani is usually combined with ferns using the haku, wili or humu-papa methods of lei making.

If you should ask the Adams kids, they would tell you that the happiest, the most beautiful, the most memorable years of their lives were those of growing up on the Island of Moloka'i. And, if you should ask them a second time, they would tell you that all children should grow up there, for then, they, too, will remember the hot, dusty, Kaunakakai days that disappeared into cool, clean, star-studded nights. They would remember the futility of being stuck in the red, winter mud at Ho'olehua and the warmth that followed the hot chocolate and postum served in the downstairs portion of Aunty and Uncle Afat's homestead house. They would feel again the salt spray and wind in their faces as they raced their horses along the beach and onto the mud flats at Kamililoa. They would recall the smarting swats across their bottoms and the scolding that followed the disappearance of mochi rice cakes and oranges from the graves at the Japanese cemetery. They would re-live the long, back-breaking hours of kiawe bean picking and the hoe hana in the pineapple fields at Kualapu'u. They would long to walk again along the causeway which leads to the pier at Kaunakakai, throwing pebbles at the alamihi and a'ama along the way, then diving off cranes, swimming and sunning at the edge of the pier. They would think of dancing again on Saturday night at the Moloka'i Community Center arrayed in the leis of their special localities. They would remember the moonlight picnics with freshly caught crabs, corn-on-the-cob and hot, charred potatoes. They would recall the thrill of catching the first he'e at Kamalō and gathering limu at Morris Point. They would remember the tī leaf slides, the beating drums heard deep in the valley at Mapulehu and the land shells that clean off the plant leaves in the mountains above Ma'alehua. They would never have forgotten Mr. Ka'ahanui of Kainalu Puko'o who came to town on Saturdays as did all the country people to buy sugar and coffee, crackers and corned beef, canned milk, flour, lard, and sundry supplies. He was a handsome man, tall and straight. His amber skin was drawn tight across his broad and strong jawed face. He always wore a red lauhala hat and it always was ornamented with a lei. Most memorable were his leis of lokelani with mei sui lan and hala with laua'e. Often I thought, "what great love this man's wife must have for him."

Today, many kinds of roses grow in Hawai'i and they are all appropriate for leis: teas, floribundas, and polyanthas. The loke-lau, green rose, and loke-wai-kahuli, a rose that starts out pink and ends up being red, thus its name, rose with changing color, are good lei materials and often sought after.

ALI'IPOE, LI'IPOE, POLOKE, CANNA, INDIAN SHOT, CANNA INDICA

It is believed that the canna, a native of tropical America, was introduced not long after the discovery of the Islands. The Hawaiians used the black seeds in their gourd rattles ('ulī'ulī and 'ūlili) and pierced and strung them for leis. It is interesting to note that the Buddhists pierced the seeds and strung them into rosaries and in the twentieth century Hawaiian Catholics used them the same way.

Sometimes the bright red and yellow flowers were strung or tied to a cord for leis.

The naturalized, wild canna produced the flowers and seeds used in the lei ali'ipoe.

KĪKĀNIA-LEI, SOLANUM ACULEATISSIMUM

By the time Hillebrand arrived in the islands, *Solanum aculeatissimum,* a native of tropical America, had become well established. This led him to believe that it was introduced before the arrival of Captain Cook. Later botanists did not agree. They believed that it had arrived in the early 1800's.

"Kīkānia" is the Hawaiianized form of the Latin word "zizanium" meaning "tares," noxious weeds. "Lei" designates its use.

The somewhat poisonous, round, orange fruits of this very thorny, perennial plant are pierced through their centers starting at the stem scar, and strung on strong cord. The lei kīkānia-lei is valued for its brilliant color and lasting quality. Breast length is best for this material since the roundness of the fruits causes the lei to roll off the shoulders if the length is longer. Moloka'i, Kalaupapa in particular, is noted for its lei kīkānia-lei.

In 1934 I was eight years old, Jo was nine and Irma was seven. This was a memorable year for us because we had been invited to a parade. Not the usual Armistice Day or Memorial Day or Kamehameha Day or Fourth of July Parade, but a special one for a special person who had come to visit

(Top to bottom): Pohā; Ali'i poe; Kīkānia

(Top to bottom): Lei pohā; Lei ali'i poe; Lei kīkānia

Wearing the Lei kīkānia (top left); Pōniu—Photo by Henry Geis (right)

Wearing the Lei pōniu—Photo by Henry Geis

Pūkāmole

Tiare

Lei pūkāmole with fuchsias

Kiele

Nani ahiahi

Lei Kiele—Photo by Henry Geis

Lei nani ahiahi with kukui flowers

Wearing the Lei Kiele—Photo by Henry Geis

ing the Lei ʻawapuhi melemele

Lei ʻawapuhi melemele

Stringing the Lei ʻawapuhi (bottom left); Lei ʻawapuhi keʻokeʻo (bottom right).

Wearing haku lei ʻawapuhi

ʻAwapuhi melemele

ʻAwapuhi keʻokeʻo

with Paul Fagan at Pu'u-o-hōkū Ranch. We were excited at the thought of the parade, any parade, while Mama and our older sisters were excited because the very special person was Warner Baxter, the famous and handsome star of motion pictures.

Lei bedecked cowboys on lei covered horses, dancers encircled with leis and children carrying more leis assembled at the site where the parade was to begin. Warner Baxter as the grand marshall led the parade through the town, a twenty-minute route if you walked very slowly. A special stage had been set up at the parade's termination point in front of the Moloka'i Market. There the movie star got off his horse and mounted the platform where he was made the Mayor of Kaunakakai and given the key to our "city." We were among the many children who placed leis about his neck and along with our parents heard for the first time, "The Cockeyed Mayor of Kaunakakai," a song written especially for this occasion by R. Alex Anderson.

After the formal ceremonies, a party was held at the Yuen's house behind the market. Dad took Irma, Jo and me and our friends, Hannah and Lily Mae, to get a closer look at the new Mayor of Kaunakakai. We looked at him and he at us. Then, in typical politician fashion, he sat Jo on his knee and bounced her a while. He bounced Irma and Hannah also, but not Lily Mae or me. At the time I guessed that he was tired and I was not offended, but years later I thought about it and wondered why he didn't. Irma, Lily Mae and I had given him nice leis while Jo and Hannah had strung the only material available to them and had presented him with a lei nioi (chili pepper lei).

R. Alex Anderson's song became popular. All the Hawaiian musicians played and sang it while the comic hula dancers had fun with it. Its popularity spread to the Mainland where according to Anderson, " . . . Baxter's Studio would not let his name be associated with the song (until later on, towards the end of his career) because they thought it sounded like a brawl with the expression 'cockeyed'. Also, for a time, NBC would not let it be played on the radio networks because they thought cross-eyed people would be offended. Later this objection was withdrawn and the song went on the air. At the time they were very strict and the expression, 'placed a green panini right under the horse's tail,' had to be changed to 'horse's mane'."

Anderson's reply to my present day inquiries confirms my recollections of that parade in 1934, and provides many facts relating to the origin of his song. He had been asked to write the song by Paul Fagan, who was then planning and preparing for Warner Baxter's visit. The details of Fagan's plans appealed to him and he wrote the song based on what Fagan told him would happen when Baxter would finally arrive at Kaunakakai. Anderson never got to the actual parade and party.

There have been one or two people since 1934, who would like to be thought of as the Mayor of that song, but Anderson states, "they were not in my mind when I wrote the song. It was purely imaginary, based on what Paul had told me, including the kīkānia lei. I don't suppose that there actually was one but it fitted the meter.

So goes traditions. Someone tells a story and someone hears it. Someone writes song and someone sings it. Someone witnesses an event and someone records it. Someone sees beauty and someone captures it in a creation of movement or of color or of form. Someone believes and the beliefs are shared. Someone establishes a practice and someone passes it on. Perhaps someone starts a tradition?

Although the people on Moloka'i, as well as those on other islands, had been making the lei kīkānia long before Anderson's song, there was no real significance attached to it until "The Cockeyed Mayor of Kaunakakai" came into being. Now some forty years later, ask any Kama'āina and he will tell you that the lei kīkānia belongs traditionally to Moloka'i.

"... He made her buck and he made her fly
All over the island of Moloka'i
You can hear the kānes and wahines cheer
As they gave him a lei of kīkānia.
And now you've heard my story
About the mayor of Kaunakakai,
All his fame and glory
on the island of Moloka'i ...."[18]

POHĀ, PA'INA, CAPE GOOSEBERRY, HUSK TOMATO, GROUND CHERRY, PHYSALIS PERUVIANA

A native of South America perhaps introduced by Vancouver, the pohā grows wild in Hawai'i on open mountain slopes at elevations of 1,500 to 4,000 feet. The yellow to orange fruits enclosed in tan papery husks was a favorite material for the lei maker who lived at the higher elevations. Parker Ranch cowboys often wore the long lasting lei pohā about their western-style hats. Each husk is peeled away from the fruit and gathered together at its base forming a kind of stem. These with the fruits attached are plaited with ferns, haku method, or tied to a center cord using the wili method of lei making.

PŌNIU, BALLOON VINE, HEARTSEED. CARDIOSPERMUM HALICACABUM

A native of tropical America, *Cardiospermum halicacabum,* a slender vine with finely subdivided leaves, small white flowers and balloon-like fruits, was used in its entirety in a lei po'o which was believed to possess the power to heal. Since the Hawaiians associated it with the curing of headaches, they called it pōniu, dizzy. The lei pōniu was placed about the head, a little was eaten and then it was cast into the sea to cure a headache. The lei was made by simply gathering lengths of the vine and twisting or loosely plaiting them together. The completed lei circled the head and the ends were wound around each other to secure it in place.

The pōniu arrived in Hawai'i soon after its discovery by western explorers. It was first collected by Gaudichaud, a French botanist, in 1819.

Today, there are Hawaiians who still believe in the healing powers of the lei pōniu. They wear the lei and eat some of it to rid themselves of headaches. They treat the headaches of their offsprings in the same manner.

PŪKĀMOLE, LYTHRUM MARITIMUM

Growing wild in the forest at about two thousand feet above sea level this rather scrubby plant with quadrangular stems, inch long leaves and tiny pink or purple flowers can easily be passed by if one is not sure of what he has to find. When cultivated, it is a beautiful plant. The young branches which may grow to a foot and a half long are stripped like maile and lengths knotted together to make the lei pūkāmole. Lei pūkāmole is seldom worn by itself. It is usually wrapped around a lei of another material. This delicate, mildly scented lei is preferred for its fragrance which is not noticed until the lei has dried out a little. It was often used in place of maile by Hawaiians of Ka'ū and the Volcano area ol Hawai'i. It is rarely seen today.

NANI AHIAHI, FOUR O'CLOCK, MARVEL OF PERU, MIRABILIS JALAPA

Between 1851 and 1871, Hillebrand noted that *Mirabilis jalapa* had escaped from the gardens and was growing wild along the roadsides. The flowers, which bloom in the late afternoon and last through the evening to sunrise of the next day, were plaited into a fern braid or tied to a cord of natural material for the lei nani ahiahi. The red, white, yellow or striped, gently scented flowers perfume the night air as it served as a gift of love for evening wear. The nani ahiahi (evening beauty) is rarely used in the contemporary lei, unless, of course you happen to spend some summer

---
[18] From a song: THE COCKEYED MAYOR OF KAUNAKAKAI by R. Alex Anderson.

Pīkake

Lei pīkake with other leis

Lei poepoe pīkake

Receiving Lei pīkake

evenings at Wailua on Moloka'i and you are driven by the scent and compelled by the simple beauty of the blossoms to haku (make) a lei. While still immature, the small textured dark seeds are sometimes strung into leis.

KIELE, GARDENIA, GARDENIA AUGUSTA

The gardenia was introduced from China in the 1830's. The fragrant white blossoms soon became a favorite with the lei maker. The calyx of each blossom along with the lower half of the flower tube is removed. The blossoms are then pierced through the center and strung on strong string or fiber (lei pololei). A common alternate is to remove only the calyx and attach the rest of the flower to a center cord with ferns and other floral material with string or fiber using the wili method of leimaking. The haku and humu-papa methods are sometimes used to make the lei kiele, but are not as popular as the kui or wili methods. As other gardenias were introduced, they too, were used in leis.

The tiare *(G. taitensis)*, a native of the Society Islands where they are also used in leis, is most often seen in leis used by the Tahitian entertainers in Hawaiian night clubs. As with other fragrant leis, Hawaiians poetically associated the lei gardenia with love and lovemaking.

"He aloha ku'u lei kiele la,
Me 'oe ke aloha bonito,
A hiki aku wau i laila la
Konikoni i ku'u pu'u wai."[19]

"A gardenia lei is my love,
Aloha bonito to you,
To whom I go
With throbbing heart."

It didn't take long for us to discover that our new home on what was then called the "Lonely Island," was really our new home on the "Friendly Island." The neighbors from down the street came to welcome us. My mother's distant relatives from Wailua and Ho'olehua came to help us get settled. The Wailua relatives were native to the island and could trace their lineage to the ruling chiefs of Moloka'i. The Ho'olehua relatives were recent transplants who had been caught up in Prince Jonah Kuhio Kalanianaole's grand scheme of rehabilitation, the Hawaiian Homes Act. They had been awarded a forty acre parcel of land with a ninety-nine year lease at a dollar a year rental.

It was Prince Kuhio's hope that a return to an agricultural existence would restore his dwindling and often destitute people to their former preeminence. So, our Ho'olehua relatives were being "rehabilitated." They found time in their busy schedule to help us to get settled at Kaunakakai and to share many precious moments of growing up on the Friendly Island.

We went hunting, fishing, picnicking, exploring and crabbing together. We shared our secrets, our hardships, our dreams, and our successes. And, when we were teenagers, we went dancing together on Saturday nights at the Ho'olehua gym or the Moloka'i Community Center. Uncle Alfred was a "dream of a dancer" and all of the girls, young and old, looked forward to dancing with him because he made even the "clunkiest" of us look like feathers floating in the slightest summer breeze. These evenings of Saturday dancing were always filled with the scent of hala, pīkake, poni mō'ī, 'awapuhi, pakalana and gardenia leis made more acute by warm dancing bodies.

As I look back on those years and try to make an assessment of the things that were worthwhile or worthless, I am often puzzled by the "rehabilitation" of our Ho'olehua relatives and others like them. They never became farmers nor did they become independent. They became lessors of sorts for they sub-leased thirty-five of their forty acres to the big pineapple companies, then went to work for these companies or for the state or county governments. They never even farmed the five acres which they kept for themselves. There were al-

[19]From a song, "HALONA," by J. Elia. P. 41 Nā Mele O Hawai'i Nei, Elbert and Mahoe.

ways problems to be solved first—getting water to the plains, planting windbreaks, finding the right crop, the right seed, projecting markets and marketing techniques, getting water!

Well, they finally got water to the Ho'olehua plains, but our relatives had long since left the homestead and had returned to the urban area from whence they came certain that their success lay in the business, professional, educational and entertainment center of the islands, Honolulu. Perhaps they were right for they now have become independent, not rich, but not destitute either. And what of those who stayed at Ho'olehua? Will they farm their lands now that the pineapple companies are phasing out? And I wonder what the philanthropic prince is thinking as he looks upon us today from the land where Kāne dwells?

'AWAPUHI KE'OKE'O, WHITE GINGER, HEDYCHIUM CORONARIUM, 'AWAPUHI MELEMELE, YELLOW GINGER, HEDYCHIUM FLAVESCENS

These large herbs, native to India, are found cultivated as well as growing wild along streams and damp, cool, roadsides. They probably were brought to Hawai'i before 1871 by the Chinese who valued them for their fragrant flowers. Hillebrand described them as "very common and occasionally found as escapes." It must have been about this time that the leimaker strung the first lei 'awapuhi ke'oke'o. They selected the flowers because of their lovely fragrance and were not concerned that the lei should last for only a little while. The fragrance lasted and the love that the lei represented was more important than the lei itself.

This is an evening lei, literally as well as figuratively. Literally, the flowers are usually gathered in the evening when they are just beginning to open. The fully matured buds are plucked from the bracts of the ginger plant and placed in a shallow pan of water until their membranous sepals pull away from their petals. The sepals are then removed and the flower stems are snipped off with thumb nail and fore-finger to about a quarter of an inch from the base of the flower. The lei'awapuhi ke'oke'o is made by using the kui method of construction. The flowers are strung on string, hau bast or banana fiber with a long needle. Each blossom is pierced through a natural hole from the tip end rather than the stem end. Several flowers are arranged on the needle with the stamens all together on one side of the needle framed by the two smaller petals of each blossom. The remaining large petal of each blossom is on the underside of the needle and ultimately the underside of the lei. This is known as a single lei.

I smiled approvingly as I watched while my husband inhaled the fragrance of the lei about his neck. He examined the single strand of delicate white blossoms and gingerly caressed it. "It's beautiful!" he said. I was pleased with his response to this gift which commemorated no special occasion and which resulted from my not being able to resist the bunches of white ginger buds wrapped in tī leaves at the little roadside stand where I had stopped to buy some papayas.

After I had bought the bundles of ginger buds, I wondered why I had squandered a whole dollar for them. I brushed the wonderment aside with an "oh, well" and as I drove home I said out loud, "I'll make a lei for Bill." For a moment my conscience was soothed. The dollar was well spent—for Bill! Then I remembered that I had married a haole guy, a typical American from Virginia who frowned upon guys who wear flowers. I brushed that memory aside with my usual "oh, well" and "I'll still make a lei for Bill. He won't be able to resist this one." I was right!

He wore the lei all evening and before going to bed, he hung it on the knob of our bedroom door. As he settled beside me in bed, he asked, "Can we grow those flowers?" "Yes," I replied. "Then," he continued, "we shall have a whole pile of them." Soon after, we planted some. Bill gathered ginger rhizomes along the road to Hana, Maui, so we could plant some outside the master bedroom window of our new home in Kāne'ohe. This was a very unusual thing for Bill to do. I am the one who digs up plants along the roadsides and he usually is the one who chides me with remarks like, "If you could dig up the whole world, I think you would take it home and plant it in your yard."

I am pleased that this should be his favorite lei, for it has always been a favorite in my family. My mother grew patches of white ginger where ever we lived, even in dry, hot Waikele on O'ahu and Kaunakakai on Moloka'i. They were always planted where they could get a lot of water, next to the wash house or the water faucets. When the flowers bloomed in the late summer and through the fall, Mama would string them on banana fiber with a coconut ni'au needle just as she did all of her childhood years at Hale'iwa, O'ahu.

When Mama was a child, she sometimes spent days visiting with great-grandpa S.K. and great-grandma Emelia at a place called, "Puna Mō'ī". Great-grandpa and great-grandma were caretakers for this country home which belonged to Lili'uokalani, the last queen of Hawai'i. On visits there, Mama would help great-grandma collect the white ginger buds and string them into leis for Lili'uokalani when she came to visit.

After Mama married my haole koa father and after their first baby came, they went to Puna Mō'ī to live with great-grandma who was then all alone. There my sister Hester Etelka Kapuhealani was born and there my father was introduced to the lei 'awapuhi ke'oke'o.

"Lei 'awapuhi, lei hiki ahiahi,
Hoa pili o maile-lau-li'i
Lana mālie iho ho'i ka mana'o
Me ka nani lei 'awapuhi."[20]

"Ginger lei, lei that comes in the evening,
Close friend of the small-leafed maile
Thinking with calm hope
Of the beauty of ginger lei."

The lei 'awapuhi ke'oke'o is also made as lei poepoe by piercing the flowers laterally through their unsnipped stems and arranging them on the needle as spokes on a wheel before passing them onto the string. The lei 'awapuhi constructed in this way is sometimes called a "double lei."

The 'awapuhi melemele, yellow ginger, *H. flavescens,* was not recorded by Hillebrand, therefore, it is believed that it was not introduced until the latter part of the nineteenth century. It too, became a valuable lei material and was treated like the 'awapuhi ke'oke'o.

Figuratively, the lei 'awapuhi ke'oke'o, made to be worn in the evening, sweetly scenting the bodies of the wearers, soon became a symbol of love and lovemaking.

Refrigeration has made storage of the buds possible. Buds may be gathered for several days and stored in tightly covered jars before using them in a lei.

Other gingers used in leis are: the Kahili ginger, *H. gardnerianum;* the shell ginger, *Catimbium speciosum;* the red ginger, *Alpinia purpurata;* and the torch ginger, *Phaeomeria speciosa.* Not in the ginger family, but commonly called "blue ginger" and used also in leis is *Dichorisandra thyrsiflora.*

PĪKAKE, ARABIAN JASMINE, JASMINUM SAMBAC

The pīkake probably was introduced by the Chinese who valued the flowers for their scent and used them for ornamentation and to flavor tea. This plant with very fragrant, white, one-inch flowers gets its Hawaiian name from Princess Kai'ulani who called it pīkake (peacock) after the peacocks that lived among the jasmine bushes in her garden. The peacocks and the jasmine were among her most prized possessions.

[20]The chorus of LEI 'AWAPUHI by Mekia Ke-alaka'i written in the 1890's. P. 73 Nā Mele O Hawai'i Nei, Elbert and Mahoe.

earing the Lei pua male

Pua male (top right); Wearing the Lei poni mō'ī (bottom left); Lei poni mō'ī (bottom right).

Lei pua male (top right); Stringing carnations (bottom left); Le
waioleka (bottom right).

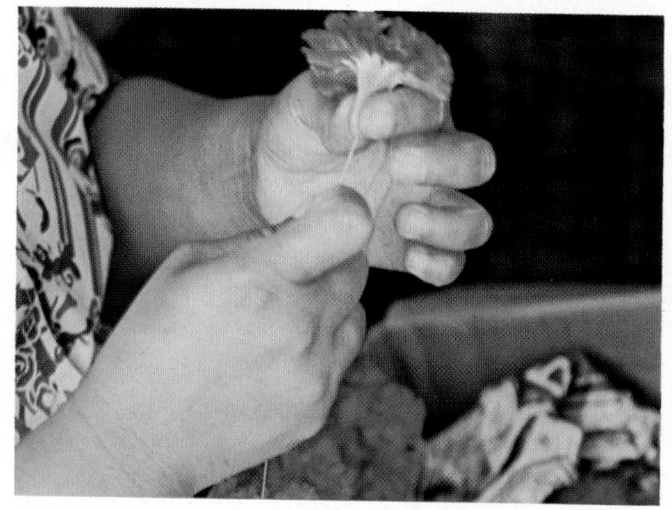

Pansies

Pakalana

Wearing a pansy lei

Mauna-loa

Pansy lei (top left); Wearing the Lei pakalana (top right); Lei pakalana (center); Lei mauna-loa (bottom left); Wearing the Lei mauna-loa (bottom right).

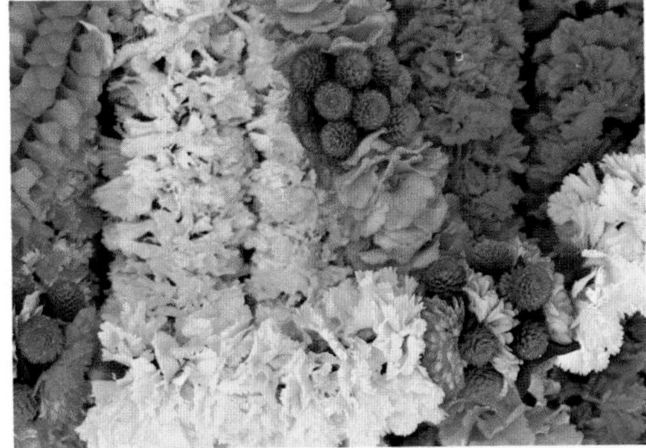

Wearing the Lei lehua haole

Left photos: (top to bottom) Lei lei-hua, Lei-hua in a mixed lei, Lei-hua & Lehua haole

Wilelaiki (top) & wearing the Lei wilelaiki (bottom)

Nani o Ōla'a, the old and new (top) & wearing the nani o Ōla'a—Photo by Henry Geis

The fragrance of the blossoms quickly caught the fancy of the leimaker and the romantic Hawaiians. At the close of the Nineteenth Century, the lei pīkake had established itself in the tradition of Hawaiian leis. It became the lei for courting, for marriage ceremonies and for honoring women in general.

The single blossoms, pīkake-lahilahi, while still buds are strung on strong thread longitudinally through the center and flower tube. A strand of pīkake-lahilahi resembles a string of ivory beads. Occasionally, the buds are strung laterally through the flower tube in the lei poepoe style. About seventy-five buds are needed to complete a single strand and about seven hundred are needed for a lei poepoe.

The buds are gathered in the evening from low growing bushes in gardens located in the dry areas of the islands. The best pīkake is to be found growing at localities, such as Kaimukī and Makaha on O'ahu, Kalama'ula and Ho'olehua on Moloka'i, Kihei and Lahaina on Maui and Puakō on Hawai'i.

For commercial use, they are refrigerated until they are ready for use to keep them from fully opening.

The pīkake that grow on the islands of Hawai'i, Maui, Moloka'i, and Kaua'i seem to be bigger and whiter than those that grow on O'ahu. Neighbor islanders say that this is due to the less crowded conditions that exists on their islands.

Today, if you are gifted with one strand of pīkake, you feel good. If you receive two strands, you feel great! Six strands, you are overwhelmed. Twelve strands, you are ecstatic. If you receive a lei poepoe, you are beside yourself!

Hawaiian pīkake growers soon found that if they wanted their bushes to frequently produce an abundance of flowers, they had to drastically prune the plants or remove all of the leaves. The leaves were removed once or twice a year and the bushes were allowed to increase in size. The leaves served as mulch for the plants. Every second or third year, the plants were pruned.

The flowers and calyxes of the star jasmine (*Jasminum multiflorum*) and the flowers and viny stems of the Chinese star jasmine (*Trachelospermum jasminoides*) are used also for leis.

"Aloha ku'u lei pīkake,
Na'u i kiss a ho'omau iho.
E lei nō au i ko aloha.
Remember, be sure and be there."[21]

"Greetings, my pīkake lei,
I will kiss you forever.
I am a garland for your love.
Remember, be sure and be there."

Irma, Jo and I would wail and weep when we were assigned the task of stripping the leaves from the pīkake bushes that Mama grew in our back yard at Kaunakakai. We used to grasp the vinelike branches by the tips in one hand and with the other snap off the leaves while slipping down the branch to its base. We loved the flowers and the fat, round buds that came after a good stripping, but we hated the chore that made them come. We all had our turn at stripping, even the younger boys, Dick, Jim, Scott, and Michael.

There were times though, when Mama did not have enough buds for the number of leis that she needed, like the time she supplied Irma's graduating class at St. Andrew's Priory with pīkake leis. In that case, she would call Lizzie Ka'ahanui and Lizzie made up the rest. Mama often called Lizzie for we often wrote home for strands of the fragrant ivory buds.

If you knew Lizzie, you would agree when I say that she was an interesting woman. She lived on a forty acre homestead close to the airport at Ho'olehua with her husband and children. She worked hard maintaining her home, and her garden patch of vegetables and pīkakes, while driving a taxi or sometimes even a pineapple hauling truck or school bus. She was always at the airport hustling for fares and she was seldom without her favorite

[21] From a song composed by J. Elia before 1930. P. 89 Nā Mele O Hawai'i Nei, Elbert and Mahoe.

pīkake in strands wrapped around the pug at the nape of her neck or draped around her shoulders. If she wasn't wearing a lei pīkake, she would tuck a pīkake-pupupu behind her ear or into her pug.

It is not the same visiting Moloka'i without first greeting Lizzie at the airport.

WAIOLEKA, VIOLET, VIOLA ODORATA

Hawaiians have always been fond of fragrant materials for leis and when the small white centered or fringed, purple, Eurasian-African, *Viola odorata* appeared in Hawai'i, they immediately constructed a lei with them to perfume their bodies and those of their loved ones. It is believed that the missionary women introduced the violets, a momento of home, sometime after 1860. Pānānā Napela Parker was said to have introduced it and the Mānā daisy, English daisy *(Bellis perennis)* to Mānā, Waimea, Hawai'i, soon after her marriage. It became a favorite lei material for the paniolos and their wives. The lei waioleka is constructed by plaiting the soft supple stems of the flowers and leaves into a braid of ferns or by attaching them to a center cord with a binding thread. Often violets are combined with other materials for leis. Waimea women also make leis of white, pink, lavender and double violets.

PUA MALE, STEPHANOTIS FLORIBUNDA PUA-HŌKŪ-HIHI, WAX PLANT, HOYA BICARINATA

Stephanotis, a native of Madagascar, and the wax plant from islands of the South Pacific probably were strung into leis before Hillebrand reported them as being well established in Hawaiian gardens, for certainly, the Hawaiians could not resist the fragrance of both flowers. Both plants are in the milkweed family and upon introduction to Hawai'i acquired very descriptive names, pua male, marry flower, because the white flowers were used in wedding bouquets, and pua-hōkū-hihi, star flower vine.

As few as twenty-five or as many as seven hundred pua male flowers are strung into a lei of forty inches. The flowers are plucked from their clusters, the calyx removed, and are strung lengthwise through the one to two inch long tubes (twenty-five flowers), or the tubes are cut short then strung the same way (seven hundred flowers). The flowers are often strung laterally through the center of the tube for a lei poepoe or are combined with other flowers in a lei wili or a lei humu-papa.

The pua-hōkū hihi are also plucked from their clusters and strung through their centers. For a lei forty-inches long, about three hundred flowers are needed.

"Ua hiki no me a'u ka moani a'ala
Ka ala o ku'u lei stephanotis pua male
Lei 'oe lei au i ka hanahano
Ku'u pua a'u i 'ano'i ai."[22]

What great joy it is when the breeze
Brings the fragrance of my lei stephanotis, the wedding flower
Honor fills our hearts, my beloved when in the presence of our cherished blossoms.

PONI-MŌ'Ī, CARNATION, DIANTHUS CARYOPHYLLUS

The Hawaiians confused the word carnation with the word coronation thus Hawaiian for carnation is poni mō'ī meaning to crown a king or queen. The missionary women of New England are credited with the introduction of this native of Eurasia sometime before Kalākaua's reign. It was a favorite of the "Merry Monarch."

With their small, fine scented flowers, they quickly became a favorite material for leis. One had red and white flowers and was called hae-Hawai'i (Hawaiian flag). Like other early imports which were dark red, very delicate pink, light red, white, magenta and very shocking pink, the hae-Hawai'i was finely scented and very popular for leis on boat

[22] From a song, PUA MALE, by John Kamealoha Almeida.

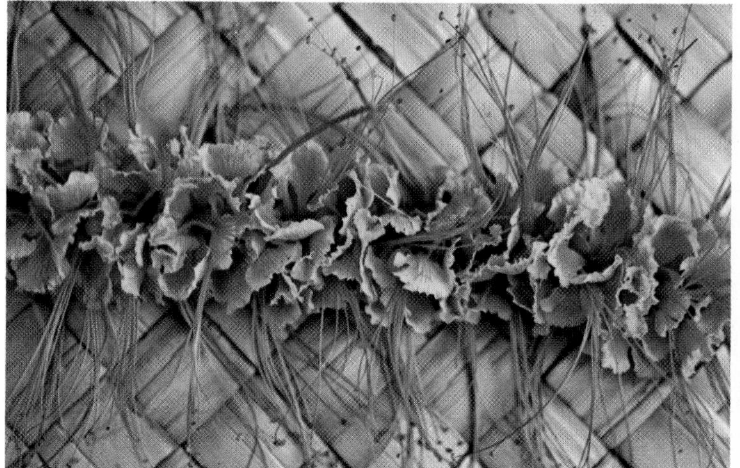

'Ōhai ali'i (top left), Lei 'ōhai ali'i (bottom left) & wearing the Lei ōhai ali'i (below)

days, graduations, proms, dates and anniversaries.

Carnations were cultivated in the Koko Crater area on O'ahu especially to meet the demands of the fast growing tourist industry. In 1900, gardens in Pauoa supplied lei sellers at the piers with carnations and other lei flowers. Japanese and Korean farmers leased small parcels of land along Lunalilo Home Road and soon their "carnation plantations" were familiar sights. Now the farms and carnations have been replaced by urban development and the commercial lei makers air ship the larger, scentless hybrids from the mainland to use in this very popular lei. The imports are usually limited to red and white. Sometimes one may find a sherbet orange, yellow, pink, or mixed red and white variety. Some carnations are still grown commercially at Kula on Maui and Waimea on Hawai'i. Of course, home gardeners raise their own carnations for their own leis. Today one hears the older Hawaiians bemoan the fact that the lei poni mō'ī are not as beautiful and not as sweetly scented as those of the turn of the century.

The white carnation lei is usually given to women and the red to the men: white being femininely pure and withdrawn—red representing masculine boldness, strength and power.

The kui method is used to make the lei poni mō'ī. The small, scented, varieties had their calyxes removed and the blossoms are pierced through the ovaries. A long (about 16") thin needle made of fishing leader wire (stainless steel) is used. The lei maker loads the needle with twelve or more flowers before passing them on to a strong string. She makes five or more such passes in order to complete a lei. For the large modern hybrid, the lei maker just slits the calyxes, and pierces the flowers through the ovaries for a single lei. For the double or triple leis that are popular with teenagers, the calyxes are left intact and the blossoms are strung as lei poepoe. Depending on the type of flowers used and the style of lei desired, sixty-five to one hundred flowers are needed to complete a lei.

Other members of the pink family are used in leis. They are poni mō'ī li'ili'i or sweet William, *D. barbatus* and *D. chinensis.*

Carnations are combined with other kinds of flowers for leis.

The lei stands at the International Airport and on Maunakea Street may have on display several leis in which carnations are strung with tuberose, plumerias, coleus, chrysanthemums, globe amaranths or orchids.

"Ano'ai eia no me a'u
Ke 'ala o ku'u lei carnation
I wili 'ia me ka maile
Moani ke 'ala i ka ihu."[23]

Greeting, it is here with me now
The fragrance of my carnation lei.
Entwined with the maile
Its scent reaches my nose.

"Ke 'ala kai hiki mai
O ku'u lei poni mō'ī
Noho 'oe a mana'o mai
Ho'i mai kāua e pili."[24]

The scent has come to me
My carnation lei
Do remember
To return to me.

"Is he really your cousin?" Bill badgered us. "I don't think he even knows you." He teased Jo and her husband Bill, Hester and her husband Bob, Irma and her husband Walla and me. "Hey, Bill McDonald," Jo commanded, "be quiet and watch the show."

It was Alfred Apaka we were hearing and watching at the Hawaiian Village Tapa Room. "Here in this enchanted place" he sang, "

[23] From a song, KU'U LEI CARNATION, by J.K. Almeida, Dec. 1956.

[24] From a song, LEI PONI MŌ'Ī, by W.J. Coelho, from Johnny Noble's Royal Collection of Hawaiian Songs, 1929. Translation by Alice Namakelua.

Agapanthus lei

Freesias (below) & Freesia lei with maile lauli'i (bottom photo)

Agapanthus in a mixed lei & Agapanthus (below)

here is where I'd rather be." He stood tall, and dark, and handsome in a very white shirt and very white trousers. He wore the red carnation lei which is now and will be forever associated with him. The song ended and he started another one, "He inoa keia no Waipi'o." He sang it for us and Bill McDonald was silent to the very end. Then he applauded with great vigor and exclaimed: "He's good; very good!" as though he had discovered him. "I don't care if he is or is not related to you, he's still good."

Alfred Apaka, "Aholo" to us, joined us at our table and in fifteen minutes we found out how his side of the family was faring while he asked of our side. We recalled some of the happy and funny moments of our childhood on the island of Moloka'i. We remembered the icy cold showers and chilling cement floors of the downstairs portion of their Ho'olehua home; the hot chocolate and freshly baked bread that followed the icy cold showers; his pineapple hauling days; our picnics and camping trips; and Pally, his sister, throwing a handful of poi, exactly as she pitched baseballs, and hitting Kealoha (the Afat's hanai cousin, but not blood related to us) smack in the mouth.

We laughed as Jo recalled that event. For some reason, Pally was perturbed with Kealoha. She had warned him, "don't you call my Aunty Lio and my Uncle John 'aunty' and 'uncle.' They are not your aunty and uncle." Kealoha persisted, not because he was spiteful, but because he had called my mother and father "aunty" and "uncle" for years. Now, all of a sudden, Pally discovered that there is no real relationship between her cousin Kealoha and the Adamses and she resents his use of "aunty" and "uncle" in addressing my mother and father. After several warnings, Pally could not contain herself. Kealoha came through our back door calling, "Uncle Jo—." He didn't finish. Pally, who was mixing poi for dinner that night, hit him smack in the mouth with a handful of pa'i 'ai. It was funny, just like a Three Stooges comedy. We laughed while Kealoha spat the poi from his mouth and wiped it from his face—not for long! Aunty Afat pushed open the swinging door from the dining room with Mama immediately behind her. You can guess the results.

Another moment of our childhood was remembered when Hester commented on Aholo's red carnation lei and he said, "can't beat the carnation leis from the Titcombs. I think these carnations come from the Mainland—no scent." The Titcombs lived at Ho'olehua, not too far from the Afats. "Now those were carnations." Aholo continued. "They were so fragrant, red and white stripped ones, light delicate pink ones; almost black, red ones; brilliant magenta ones and Kaiser pink ones." He could not resist a plug for his boss, Henry J. and besides, that is exactly what they were—wild pink—Henry J. Kaiser pink. (If you lived in Honolulu during the period of the Henry J. Kaiser influence, you'll remember Kaiser pink.)

Aholo's group gathered on the little stage. The steel guitarist "twanged" a couple of notes. It was a code, I'm sure. The message read, "okay, Alfred, pau rest, time to entertain."

PĀNEKI, PO'O-KANAKA, PANSY, VIOLA TRICOLOR

Another plant material the missionary women probably introduced is the pansy, a native of Europe, which now grows in the cooler areas on all the islands. In 1851 Jack Purdy introduced it to Waimea on Hawai'i and gave it the name po'o-kanaka, human face. Only the people of the district of Kohala, in which Waimea is located, use this name. Other islanders use pāneki from the English word pansy. The pansy thrived in the cool brisk climate of Waimea and by the turn of the century it had become a favorite material for hat leis of the Hawaiian paniolo, cowboy. Today, Hawaiians throughout the State associate the pansy lei with the paniolo and their women of Waimea, Kohala, Hawai'i.

The women of Waimea use the haku (mount in a braid) method for making the pansy lei.

(Top to bottom) Tuberose; Pua kīkā; mākāhala.

(Top to bottom) Lei tuberose; Lei pua kika; Lei mākāhala

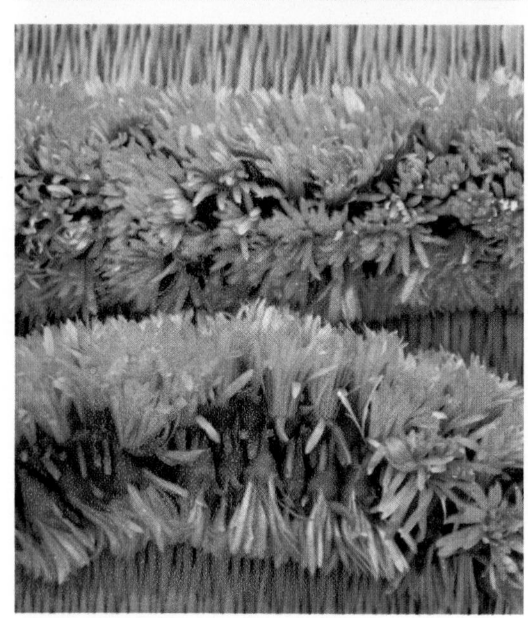

(Top to bottom) Orange ʻākulikuli; Pink ʻākulikuli; Lei ʻākulikuli.

(Top to bottom) Wearing the lei pua kika and the lei ʻākulikuli; Wearing the Lei mākāhala.

Usually blue forget-me-nots and white or lavender sweet alyssum, pink English daisy *(Bellis perennis)*, and the young aromatic leaves of the maile-haole *(Myrtus communis)* are added. These materials all have soft and supple stems which are most appropriate for braiding with palapalai fern. About three hundred fifty to four hundred pansies are needed for a lei ā'ī (neck lei).

PAKALANA, CHINESE VIOLET, TELOSMA CORDATA

"Pakalana' is the name that the Hawaiians originally gave to the *Michelia alba*, the white champak. It was derived from the Chinese, pak-lan, meaning "white flower." Marie C. Neal is correct in suggesting that the name is misapplied to the *Telosma cordata*, but through common usage "pakalana" is now an established name for *T. cordata*.

T. cordata, a slender vine native to Southern Asia was probably introduced by the Chinese in the last quarter of the nineteenth century. It is cultivated in gardens today, as it was long ago in China and India, especially for its fragrant yellow-green flowers.

Hawaiians string the half-inch flowers into leis by piercing them longitudinally, through their centers or laterally through their sides. One hundred thirty-five or 140 flowers are needed for one strand; but many strands are preferred. Today, the blossoms, which grow in clusters, are picked from the vines over several days and stored in covered glass containers in refrigerators until enough have been collected to make several strands of lei pakalana. The vines produce flowers during the summer months, often a little earlier or a little later so that the lei pakalana appears at spring graduations, summer dates, summer weddings, and fall farewells. Like other fragrant flower leis, even in modern times, the lei pakalana is associated with love and lovemaking.

The lei pakalana can be revived after being worn all evening to last through the next day or two by sprinkling it and then shaking it free of water and storing it in a plastic bag or glass container in the refrigerator. "Auwe," the oldtimers would wail when they discovered that we moderns were trying our utmost to preserve forever this very temporary momento of a very special gesture and occasion.

MAUNA-LOA, SEA BEAN, DIOCLEA WILSONII, MAUNA-LOA, CANAVALIA CATHARTICA

The plant the Hawaiians first called mauna-loa *(Dioclea wilsonii)* probably was introduced during the first half of the Nineteenth Century. A native of tropical South America, it became naturalized in the lower dry areas on all islands where the Hawaiians collected the blue or purple flowers for leis. A later introduction *(Canavalia cathartica)* acquired the name "maunaloa" because of the similarity in flowers. The newer mauna-loa, an annual vine, which is found cultivated as well as growing wild in the low lands on all the major islands is native to East Africa and Polynesia and probably was introduced in the last quarter of the Nineteenth Century. Early in the Twentieth Century, lei women along the Honolulu waterfront grew the vines in their Pauoa, Pālama, and Kalihi gardens. The pink pealike blossoms were strung into long-lasting, beautiful leis. The lei mauna-loa was popular with the kama'aina who travelled inter-island on the little ships as well as the malihini who arrived to visit the islands on the big ocean liners. Both mauna-loa leis are seldom seen today.

The blossoms are gathered early in the morning before the warm sun causes them to burst open. They are usually strung by piercing them laterally through the ovaries with a long needle. The unopened blossoms are arranged on the needle with the banner wing and keels alternating from side to side (kui lau). After several blossoms have been arranged on the needle, they are passed on to strong thread. Several passings are made until the lei is long enough for head or neck leis. The blossoms are then forced open, one banner at a time, until all are laying flat in the center of lei. The lei is finally rolled into a flat cylindrical ball for carrying or storage until ready for use.

Everyone has his own special cure for the hiccups. My mother wetted a piece of newspaper, about an inch square, with her tongue then placed it between the eyebrows in the middle of the forehead of the hiccupping child. It seemed to work. I guess we concentrated so hard on that annoying piece of paper that we forgot we had hiccups. Mama once told me jokingly that this was a family secret passed down to her from great grandma Emelia. I accepted it, but years later I began to wonder about a lot of things that my mother did or told us about.

I wondered why this woman who was determined to rear her family the way the American woman did, to make them "civilized" and to educate them so they could live and compete in the white man's world, would sometimes do some typically Hawaiian things. When we suffered with sore throats, she made us chew on 'uhaloa. She massaged our noses when we were babies so that they would not be 'ūpepe (flattened). She would not allow us to sweep anything out of the house after dark. And for every special occasion she taught us to honor and to show our love with a lei.

It was not unusual for my mother to string a lei for my father. Sometimes it was a weekly thing. If the lei material did not last the week, she would string two leis a week or three. We were all sure that she did this not just to decorate my father's hat and to keep him in style with the other luna (supervisor) types that worked on the ranches and pineapple plantations. We were certain that for my mother, every day with my father was special and the leis that she gave expressed her love and respect for him. My father knew this, so he wore the leis on his lauhala or cane hat with great pomp and circumstance.

I can remember riding along with my father in the company's Ford pickup truck to Puko'o and points beyond. He drove the island once monthly to collect the rental fees for the telephones and once in a while he would select one or two of us to ride along with him. On such occasions, my father was sure to wear a lei and he was always in good voice. Together we would sing from one house to another, "Skinamarinka dink ka dink, Skinamarinka do, I love you . . . I love a pretty Maui girl who lives at Waikapū . . ." I remember once when we stopped at the Lamauna's house and I watched my father walk down the path in his khaki riding pants, laced to the knee boots, palaka shirt and lauhala hat bedecked with a lavender-pink maunaloa lei. How handsome he was!

Most of the larger pealike blossoms and some blossoms with prominent lips are strung in the kui lau style resulting in the use of the term "maunaloa style" by present day Hawaiians. Examples are the erythrinas (native and introduced), the strongylodons (jade vine and nuku-'i'iwi) and the *Vanda* 'Agnes Joaquim'.

LEI-HUA, LEHUA-PEPA, BOZU, GLOBE AMARANTH, GOMPHRENA GLOBOSA

A native of tropical America, this popular annual with white, yellow, pink, red, violet or variegated papery-like flowers has long been established in Hawaiian gardens where it has acquired a number of local names.

The Hawaiians called it by two descriptive names: lei-hua, ball lei and lehua-pepa, paper lehua *(Metrosideros)*. Island Japanese called it bozu, bald head, while those of us who mastered pidgin called it "bola head," bald head.

No matter what name was used, the blossoms still made beautiful, long lasting leis which are often seen hanging in the lei stands at the Honolulu International Airport today. Sometimes the lehua-pepa is strung with plumerias, tuberoses, marigolds and other flowers.

LEHUA-HAOLE, CALLIANDRA INAEQUILATERA

The Hawaiians called the calliandra lehua-haole because the blossoms were similar in form and color to the native lehua *(Metrosideros)* and because it was not a native. Because of this look-alike quality, the lehua-haole is often used as a substitute for the lehua. Delicate, feathery, short-lived leis are made from the red and white blossoms of this native of Bolivia. The scentless flowers are pierced through the centers and strung on strong thread. The lei lehua-haole is an invention of the first quarter of the Twentieth Century. An earlier introduction, C. *haematomma,* having smaller red flowers was sometimes used for leis.

WILELAIKI, NANI-O-HILO, CHRISTMAS BERRY, SCHINUS TEREBINTHIFOLIUS

This native of Brazil probably was introduced at the end of the Nineteenth Century or at the beginning of the Twentieth Century. By 1930 it had established itself in the Hawaiian environment where it thrived in the waste lands and where the red berries of the female trees were used by the natives as substitute for holly berries in wreaths at Christmas time. Red berries which are gathered in November and hung in a shaded place to dry for use during the holiday season for wreaths as well as leis. According to Marie C. Neal, the Hawaiian name, wilelaiki, originated with Willie Rice, a politician, who often wore a hat lei of the berries. The red berries were never very popular for leis, but recently, the lei wilelaiki seemed to be experiencing a renaissance as it is seen on many hats during the Christmas season.

NANI-Ō-OLA'A, ŌLA'A BEAUTY, TORENIA, TORENIA ASIATICA, T. FOURNIERI

Torenia asiatica arrived in the Islands sometime during the last quarter of the Nineteenth Century. It preceded its close relative *T. fournieri* and became established in the area of Ōla'a beauty or nani-o-Ōla'a. During spring roadsides and in the fields, thus the name Ōla'a beauty of nani-o-Ōla'a. During spring and summer excursions on horseback to what was then the country, natives gathered the wild flowers and plaited the supple stems into a braid of ferns. The violet-colored leis adorned their pāpale (hats) for their return trip to Hilo after the day's end.

Today, the Ōla'a beauty is still found growing wild along the roadsides and in the fields or Ōla'a, but natives of Ōla'a and other Hawaiian communities use *T. fournieri* more often in the lei nani-o-Ōla'a since packets of seeds can easily be purchased in city stores or through mainland seed catalogues and since the flowers of *T. fournieri* are larger and more showy.

The lei nani-o-Ōla'a closely resembles the pansy lei. Sometimes the flowers are strung in lei poepoe style. The difference between the torenias is a slight variation in color. *T. asiatica* is predominately shades of voilet, while *T. fournieri* is shades of blue-voilet with a yellow spot. Both are natives of southern Asia.

'ŌHAI-ALI'I, PRIDE OF BARBADOS, DWARF POINCIANA, CAESALPINIA PULCHERRIMA

Caesalpinia pulcherrima, a native of tropical America was introduced early in the 1800's. It became established in Hawai'i quickly as it had in many other tropical countries before its introduction here. The red and yellow blossoms with conspicuous stamens impressed the Hawaiians who named it 'ōhai-ali'i, royal 'ōhai. Usually the blossoms are strung lei poepoe. Each flower is pierced laterally through the ovary and arranged in a circle. Often they are plaited with ferns or are attached to a cord with a binding thread. A pure yellow form also is used for leis.

FREESIA, FREESIA REFRACTA

Native to South America, the freesia, a member of the iris family, is often called by a misnomer, "chinese lily," by the people who grow them in the high, cooler areas of Hawai'i. The deep yellow, cream or white flowers which often have purple edges and throats are borne on low growing herbaceous plants. The fragrant, tubular, funnel-shaped, curved flowers bloom in the months of March, April, and May.

Purple, pink and red hybrids also are grown in Hawaiian gardens but are not as common a lei material as the more prevalent cream colored kinds. Freesias are strung lengthwise through their centers. Two hundred seventy-five flowers are needed for a lei thirty-eight to forty inches long. Sometimes they are added in bunches to a lei wili or lei haku.

AFRICAN LILY, LILY OF THE NILE, AGAPANTHUS AFRICANUS

The agapanthus grows best in the high, cool regions of the islands where the blue or white flowers are popular for quickly strung leis. The flowers are funnel shaped, from one to two inches long, and are borne in large heads on stoutish stalks. It is native to Africa.

The flowers are sometimes attached by their stems to a center cord for a lei wili or to a braid of ferns for a lei haku.

Other imported lilies are used by the Hawaiian lei maker, but not as often as the agapanthus. These include: the leaves and flowers of the New Zealand Flax *(Phormium tenax);* leaves from various asparagus, *Asparagus officinalis* (the edible kind), *A. setaceus* (the flat fern-type), *A. densiflorus* (the hanging basket variety), *A. racemosus, A. africanus, A. falcatus;* fragrant white flowers of the lily-of-the-valley *(Convallaria majalis).*

KUPALOKE, TUBEROSE, POLIANTHES TUBEROSA

A member of the amaryllis family, the tuberose, a native of Mexico, is grown in Hawai'i especially for the lei makers whose stands line the entrance to the airport and Maunakea Street in Chinatown. The white, very fragrant flowers are pierced lengthwise through their centers then passed on to strong thread for the lei kupaloke. Often the flowers are combined with carnations, vanda orchids, globe amaranths, chrysanthemums and others. The leis are favorites of island visitors. Rarely the flowers are pierced through sides for a lei poepoe.

Other members of the amaryllis family are sometimes used in leis: the red-orange funnel shaped flowers of the clivia *(Clivia miniata);* the white and yellow zephyr flowers *(Zephyranthes spp.);* the white flowers of the Brisbane lily *(Eurycles amboinensis)* and the Amazon lily *(Eucharis grandiflora);* and the floral tubes of the spider lily *(Pancratium littorale, Crinum giganteum* and *C. asiaticum).*

Auhea wale 'oe e ke 'ala tuberose
He moani 'a'ala i ke ano ahiahi
Ua like me ka lau wabine
I ka hoʻoheno i ka poli pili pa'a[25]

Where are you sweet fragrance of the tuberose
Wafted fragrance at eventide
Like that of the verbena leaf
It appeals to one's inner most feeling.

MĀKĀHALA, ORANGE CESTRUM, CESTRUM AURANTIACUM

Three shrubs of the tomato family, *Cestrum aurantiacum, C. diurnam,* and *Nicotiana glauca* were called mākāhala by the Hawaiians and all three were used in leis. *C. aurantiacum,* however, is the most popular of the three for lei making and is most often called by its Hawaiian name, mākāhala. A native of Guatamala, it was introduced prior to 1871. It grows well in cool Nu'uanu Valley, Kula, Maui, Kona mauka, Waiohinu, and Waimea, Hawai'i. The golden orange, inch long blossoms are

[25] From a song, KE ALA TUBEROSE, by Joseph Ae-a.

snipped in half. The base ends of the tubular flowers are cast aside while the remaining parts are strung longitudinally through the centers. About one hundred flowers make a strand. Six or more strands were twisted together in a rope for the neck. Sometimes the flowers are pierced laterally through the tubes and arranged as a lei poepoe.

"Ei aku nei paha o ka lani
I ke kui, lei kamakahala
Wili 'ia me ka 'awapuhi
Onaona i ka lau na'ena'e."[26]

Here perhaps is the heaven
Sew the mākāhala lei
Entwine with the ginger
The na'ena'e leaves are fragrant.

PUA KĪKĀ, CIGAR FLOWER, CUPHEA IGNEA

Many hundreds of blossoms are strung in various geometric patterns to create the lei pua kīkā. As is the case with the making of many leis, the gathering and preparing of the pua kīkā for stringing consumes more time than the actual construction of the lei. The three-fourths inch tubular blossoms are gathered from the small shrubs. About 2,000 are needed to make a lei 'ā'ī. Two kinds of pua kīkā are grown by the lei makers. One type has flowers with deep red-orange tubes and dark bands at the white mouths. The other type differs by having almost white tubes. The tubular flowers are pierced laterally through a point half way between their swollen base and their mouths. They are arranged on the needle as spokes on a wheel by grouping the swollen red-orange bases and the dark and white mouths to create various patterns. The flowers are then passed on to thread. A greater number of geometric patterns were created by combining the two types of pua kīkā.

The lei pua kīkā did not become popular until the early 1900's although the plants were found in Hawaiian gardens some twenty-five years earlier. Oldtime Hawaiians of Waimea, Hawai'i remember their mothers stringing the leis for special occasions.

[26] From a song, NANI NU'UANU, by Kau'i Wilcox.

'ĀKULIKULI-LEI, ICE PLANT, LAMPRANTHUS GLOMERATA

A low growing succulent, native to Africa, cultivated in Hawaiian gardens at elevations of 1,000 feet or more; a common garden plant in such areas as Waimea, Hawai'i; Ho'olehua, Moloka'i; and Kula, Maui. Leaves are narrow and thick and flowers are iridescent pink, rose, orange, white, red, magenta or yellow. The light pink and rose varieties are most common and have been used in leis since their introduction. The other varieties introduced after 1940, the yellow one being the latest, are also used in leis. The orange 'ākulikuli is said to leave a stain on clothes.

The kui method is preferred for making the lei 'ākulikuli. Blossoms are pierced through the centers and strung singly on strong thread or more often pierced laterally through the stem just below the ovary and are arranged in a half or full circle on the needle then passed on to the thread. The latter method of arranging the flowers in a full circle by piercing them through their stems is called "lei poepoe." In modern times this method of stringing is often called "'ākulikuli style" and can be very misleading when used to describe a lei of ginger blossoms constructed this way as "'ākulikuli-ginger lei." It would be more accurate to describe this kui style as "lei poepoe" no matter what kind of material is used. As the blossoms close at night and as they are easier to handle this way, the lei maker gathers them in the evening or during the early morning before they open. The blossoms are not set in water as the lei maker prefers working with soft, pliable stems rather than brittle ones. It takes 500 blossoms if strung by fives to complete a lei for the neck (lei 'ā'ī) or about 370 blossoms for a head (lei po'o) or hat lei (lei pāpale).

The Hawaiians called this African native "'ākulikuli" because this is the term for all succulents and "lei" because of its use. The lei 'ākulikuli lasts beautifully for two or three days with little or no care.

One morning in June 1975 while I was driving my son David to his summer job, I listened to a discussion on the radio between an early morning disc jockey and several telephone callers concerning the new hydrofoils and the projected inter-island passenger service. Callers were expressing doubt about the predicted regularity of service and the claims made by the company that their hydrofoils would be able to weather the Moloka'i (Ka'iwi) Channel with ease. "What about twenty feet waves? And fifty feet waves?," some caller asked. The jockey said, "call the company." The caller did and reported back, "the company official said, 'we stay home!'" I chuckled to myself.

Last night at a dinner party, Bill, my mechanic-sailor-sport fisherman-husband was involved in a similar discussion. He said with great authority and much experience, "oh, sure, they'll be able to cross the Ka'iwi Channel with ease and most of the time they will be above the water, but 'Alenuihāhā, well, that's a different story. They can't make it all the way across, airborne. They'll sail like regular ships—unless they leave Lahaina, go way to the south and avoid the channel—from Maui straight across to Kailua, Kona, they'll take a dirty licking like any other boat." I chuckled to myself last night also, remembering some thirty years ago when travel between the islands was by boat and there were small waves and big waves and times when we stayed at home a day or two longer. I chuckled even more when I remembered times when my air flight was grounded. The chuckling ceased when I asked myself, "Hey, where are we going in a hurry?" It's progress.

Progress? Is it really? I travelled the Ka'iwi Channel regularly on an ocean craft in the late 1930's through early September of 1941. That was the only way we could get to school and back again. Hester, John, Jo and I did it as did all the other kids on Moloka'i who attended school in Honolulu.

At the beginning of the school year and at the end of the Christmas and Spring holidays, we would board the S.S. Wai'ale'ale or the S.S. Hualalai or the S.S. Humu'ula or the S.S. Hawai'i to return to school in Honolulu. First we gathered at the pier in Kaunakakai, around midnight. There were lots of luggage and lots of leis—iridescent rose and light pink 'ākulikuli, fragrant pīkake and spicy sweet carnations from Ho'olehua; pungent hala, mountain fresh gingers from Mana'e; gentle maile lauli'i from Maunahui. The night air was chilly. Mothers reminded children to do this and to do that, while fathers gathered in a bunch to smoke and discuss the affairs of the day.

Hanky Yamamoto jockeyed the motor launch into position at the end of the pier. During the summer months, Hanky moved it quickly into place, but after the Christmas and Spring holidays, the launch pitched and lurched. The waves tossed it high above the pier, then dropped it way below the pier. Fathers helped us in. "Okay, now." they shout! Sometimes Hanky had to circle beyond the pier and at the right moment, he would pull up to the pier and more passengers would jump on. "Bye, bye," we call between pitching and lurching and circling and parting tears.

The ship's stewards help us off the launch and on to the gangway. Hanky circled again and again and finally all are aboard. Usually our parents would have booked us for deck passage—young people can take the salt and open air. We are provided with mattresses and blankets, so we may sleep the rest of the night. We never do. We talk and visit and eat until we arrive in Honolulu the next morning.

Sometimes we meet school friends from Maui or Hawai'i on the same ship. Sometimes we gather in the stateroom of one of our friends whose parents are rich enough to afford one, to press on buzzers for food service. Sometimes we get seasick be-

Wearing the Lei pua kenikeni

Pua kenikeni

Pua kalaunu

Wearing the Lei pua melia (bottom left); Pua melia (bottom right).

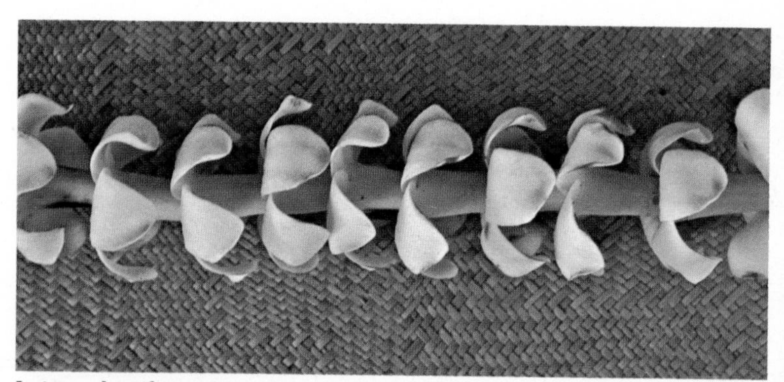

Lei pua kenikeni

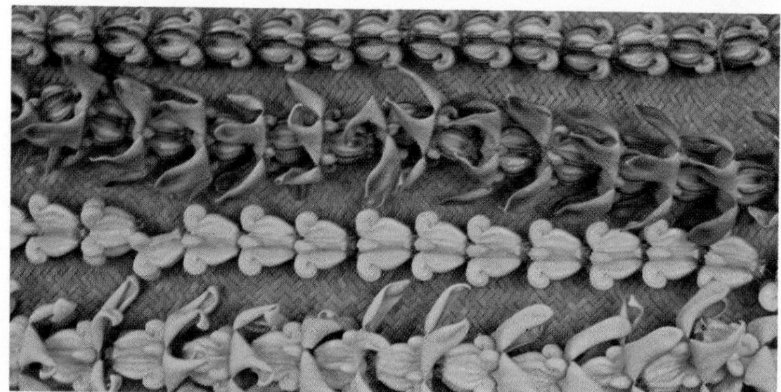

Lei pua kalaunu

Wearing the Lei kalaunu (top right); Lei pua melia (bottom left); Wearing the Lei 'umi 'umi o Dole (bottom right).

Wearing the Lei kukuna-o-ka-lā

Kukuna-o-ka-lā

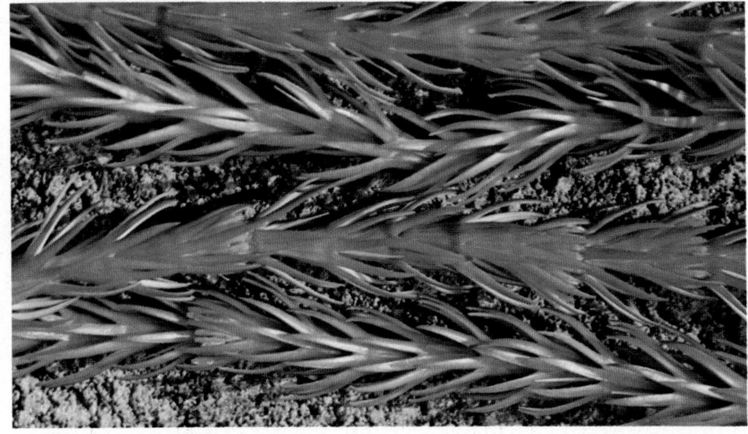
Lei kukuna-o-ka-lā

Alahe'e haole

Lei alahe'e haole

Banyan leaf lei

Wearing the Lei alahe'e haole

Wearing a mixed neck lei (top); Wearing head and hat leis (bottom).

A mixed lei with daisies; A mixed lei with bougainvillea; A mixed lei with the cup and saucer flowers.

cause of a rough ocean and often from the sickening scent our flower leis acquire on an ocean voyage. We put the leis in a place where we can't smell them. We never throw them away. Tomorrow when the seasickness subsides and we arrive at either Pier 10 or 13, and when we are at school, we will wear our leis with boastful pride so all the Honolulu kids can see and wish that they were from the country too.

When we leave Honolulu for home, the only difference lies in the parting scene. We are driven to the pier in the school station wagon. A relative is always there to present us with a lei. Most often it is a lei poni mō'ī, a very light delicate pink one, or a shocking magenta one or a deep red one and always with sprigs of maiden hair tucked in here and there.

We board the ship right from the pier. We lean over the railings calling our farewells. Our stomachs ache with anxiety. We're going home! "Aloha a hui hou," someone calls up to us.

Today, we travel inter-island by air; so quickly that there is not time for the lei anymore.

PUA KENIKENI, FAGRAEA BERTERIANA

A native to the South Pacific Islands, the pua tree, as it is known there, was introduced by Jarrett P. Wilder in the late 1800's. It is believed that the pua tree was first planted in Maunawili, O'ahu. The fragrant blossoms attracted many residents of O'ahu's windward area and soon the pua became the flower of Kāne'ohe. Because the flowers, at one time, were sold for ten cents apiece, the Hawaiians called it, "pua kenikeni," ten cents flower.

Few pua kenikeni trees are found outside of windward O'ahu. There, gardeners keep them pruned and wide spreading so flowers are in easy reach when gathering them.

The fragrant tubular flowers bloom a creamy white and by the second day, they change to a subtle orange. They are usually strung on thick lengths of banana fiber, knitting yarn, or one-inch wide bandage. The base half of the flower tube is usually cut off before stringing. Sometimes the flowers are combined with other materials in a lei wili.

"No ka pua kenikeni ko'u ho'ohihi
Ke 'ala ho'oheno i ku'u poli.
Onaona i ka ihu ke honi aku
A ke kēhau a'e hali mai nei."[27]

My desire is for the pua kenikeni
Its fragrance reaches within my bosom.
Inhale its fragrance
Brought here by the dew.

"No ka lei aloha, lei pua keni keni
Ko'u hia 'ai a me ko'u ho'ohihi."[28]

For the beloved lei, lei pua kenikeni

MELIA, PLUMERIA, FRANGIPANI, PLUMERIA RUBRA, P. OBTUSA, P. EMARGINATA

It is believed that William Hillebrand introduced the first plumerias in the late 1800's as one of the plant materials he gathered on his trip to the Orient as Commissioner of Immigration for the Kingdom of Hawai'i. This first of many kinds of plumerias was *P. rubra,* a native of tropical America which had been established in South Asian gardens by the Spaniards who travelled between Acapulco and Manila during the last half of the Fourteenth Century. Otto Degener credits Mrs. Paul Neumann with the introduction of the red plumeria from Mexico about 1871. Dr. Harold Lyon is credited for the introduction of *P. obtusa,* a native of the West Indies, commonly called the Singapore plumeria, in 1931 from Singapore. Hawaiian hybridizers produced other varieties. Today, there are a number of pinks, yellows, whites and reds. There is a plumeria that smells like apricots which islanders call the rainbow and one which is red and white striped which is called hae-Hawai'i, Hawaiian flag; the Scott Pratt, a deep red and the Wilcox with very large

[27] From a song, PUA KENIKENI, by Flora Waipa.
[28] From a song, LEI PUA KENIKENI, by J.K. Almeida.

blossoms. All are used in leis of contemporary times.

The melia did not become a popular lei material in Hawai'i until about the 1940's. Soon after its introduction, cuttings were planted in graveyards where they thrived with little or no care, hence the common name graveyard plumeria, developed. This association with death led many Hawaiians to shun the melia as a lei material. However, tourism and its demands for a flower lei for every tourist that visited the islands led to the use of the easy to grow, abundant, easy to string, fragrant, long lasting plumeria for leis. Today, only the oldtimers refuse to wear the lei melia. The plumeria has become so popular that almost every home, especially on O'ahu, will have one or two plants to take care of the family's need for leis for their mainland friends, for graduations, for parties, for conventions, and for decorating graves.

Flowers are abundant during the summer months at the peak of the tourist season. Plants bloom best where all the tourist centers are located in the dry, warm lee coastal areas of all the major islands. Thus, every tourist that has ever visited the islands remembers the lei melia as being the predominant lei of the land and many wonder why islanders value "a bunch of leaves," the lei maile, over the fragrant, colorful, plumeria lei.

The lei melia is made by stringing the flowers lengthwise through their centers usually with the long leader wire needle patterned after the old nī'au needle and developed by the lei sellers on the waterfront in the early 1900's through their association with the fisherman. If many leis are to be made, the needle is lubricated with vaseline to keep the milky sap of the plumerias from accumulating on it. Sometimes plumerias are strung lei poepoe style and other times the petals are torn apart then strung. The latter way is not very appropriate for the material since in a matter of minutes after it is made, the petals begin to shrink and the wearer of the lei is left with a string around his neck and a bunch of shrivelled petals on his chest.

I boarded an American Airlines plane at Love Field, Texas and now was sitting in the Pan American Terminal in San Francisco waiting to make a connection with my flight to Honolulu. My stomach churned with excitement, the same anxiety I had always felt and would probably always feel when I was going home. I had just finished college. It was February, 1948. It was night and while I sat there, I thought of home. The war, World War II, had ended while I was away and I was sure that things would be a lot different than when I was home last in August of 1944. One good thing, I thought, there'll be no gas masks to carry about and there'll be no gas rationing, no rationing of any kind! It will be warm and sunny, but if it should be raining, it will be warm rain. The kind of rain in which one goes barefoot and splashes around. The kind of rain that you don't run from, but instead, drink in with upturned face. Not a sad rain, but a happy rain. The sunshine rain!

They announced the departure of my PanAm strato-cruiser. I boarded it, removed my gloves, hat and coat, for the last time I had hoped, and bundled up with a blanket. I looked out the window for something interesting to see. There was nothing. It was dark and raining. The lights everywhere shimmered, reflected and bounced off wet pavement and wet buildings. Burrrr! I shuddered and pulled the blanket up to my chin. I was beginning to feel the weariness of the long flight and I still had eight hours to go. I dozed a bit and thought of home again.

I'll arrive in Honolulu early tomorrow morning. Someone will be there to meet me. Perhaps Hester or Irma or maybe even John will be there. I'll spend the day there and the next morning there'll be a thirty-minute flight to Moloka'i.

I smiled, a wistful smile, as I remembered the first flight that we ever made from Honolulu to

Moloka'i. It was a week after December 7, 1941. All the kids at school had been sent home a little earlier than usual for the Christmas holidays. The O'ahu kids went home before those of us who came from the "outer" islands. School officials delayed our departure until they were positive that inter-island travel was safe again. While we stayed at school, we cleaned and scrubbed and made beds in preparation for further attack and a possible change to an evacuation center.

When it was safe, they flew Jo and me and all the other kids home.

There were no leis and no beautiful fragrances, no kisses from relatives, no "aloha a hui hou." Only austere, sober and quiet faces. There wasn't even the excitement of a first airplane ride. It was war!

When we arrived in Homestead Field at Ho'olehua, the gusting winds lifted our dresses high over our heads as we came out of the top of the airplane and down a gangway to the ground. Mama and Dad were there.

I dozed until the stewardess tapped me on the shoulder and said, "Miss, we'll be landing at Honolulu International Airport in thirty minutes." We landed and there were lights shimmering, reflecting and bouncing off wet pavement and wet buildings. It was dark and it was raining, warm rain.

I ran through it and into the terminal building. There was no one there, just some guy pushing a broom around! Immediately, disappointment and sadness engulfed me. Then, I thought, "this must not be the place. Someone would be here if it were the right place!" It was the right place! There was Hester coming through the wide doorway with an umbrella in one hand and a plumeria lei in the other. No words spoken. Just the giving and receiving of a lei, a kiss and an embrace.

The plumeria lei was not always sweet for me. It was sometimes sad. Many years later I visited my mother, who had become an invalid, in a hospital. I was wearing and carrying several plumeria leis given to me at a luncheon and I wanted to share them with her. She saw me coming, then abruptly turned her face from me and before I could say anything, she ordered me to get rid of the leis. I didn't understand, but I got rid of them and returned to her bedside whereupon, she admonished me for still smelling like plumerias and promptly dismissed me.

Later in the day I mentioned her strange reaction to my brother Dick and he, in his all knowing, very wise way said, "hey, stupid, have you forgotten that the plumeria is the 'make man's flower'—dead man's flower?" I had blundered.

PUA KALAUNU, CROWNFLOWER, CALOTROPIS GIGANTEA

The lavendar variety of the crownflower was introduced before the white in about 1888. It was a favorite of Lili'uokalani, last of the reigning monarchs, and did not become popular until after her death in 1917. According to Marie C. Neal, the white crownflower, a native of India to the East Indies, was introduced about 1920. The crownflower is more or less poisonous. The milky sap sometimes irritates the skin and if ever dropped into the eyes can cause severe inflammation and pain.

Crownflower leis became popular in the late 1920's. The flowers which have a pleasing odor are usually strung longitudinally through the centers for the lei pua kalaunu. Sometimes the "petals" or calyxes are removed and only the flower crowns are strung. Less frequently, only the petals are strung into a lei. Rarely one will find a lei pua kalaunu which has been constructed by first casting aside the petals, then tearing the crowns into five pieces and finally, stringing these torn apart pieces into many strands. This finished lei has the appearance of many strands of tiny white or lavendar shells. Sometimes the flowers are strung back to back and at other times they are strung lei poepoe. Sometimes many strands are twisted together to form a rope. Sometimes the tops of the flower crowns are cut off and just the bottoms are strung. The leimaker found that the kui method of leimaking was most appropriate for the crownflower, but she did not rule out the other methods of lei construction. For the lei po'o and the lei pāpale, the humu-papa method was often used and since the stems of the crownflower were long enough and supple enough, the wili and haku methods were also used though not as frequently as the kui method.

In the 1940's, the lei pua kalaunu and the lei pīkake inspired craftsmen. The results were ivory replicas which were sold in many leading jewelry shops. So realistic were the replicas, they were often mistaken for the originals until the lack of scent gave them away. More recently plastic replicas are being sold in island stores.

Crownflowers are found growing best at the lower elevations and the dry, hot areas of the islands. They do well and are often used for leis at such places as Kawaihae and Puakō on Hawai'i, Kihei and Lahaina on Maui, Kaloaloa, Waimanalo, Nānākuli, Wai'anae and Makaha on O'ahu, Kekaha, Waimea, Po'ipū on Kaua'i; Kaunakakai, Kamililoa and Kalama'ula on Moloka'i.

'Aia i ka laulā me ka loa
'Ike 'ia e ka nani o Kaloaloa
Hiehie nō 'oe me kou nani
Ua wehi i ka lei pua kalaunu."[29]

There in the broad wide space
Is seen the beauty of Kaloaloa
You are grand with your beauty
Bedecked with the crownflower lei.

When summer came to an end, Mama would keep all of us girls away from the beaches and out of bathing suits. This was a regular end of summer ritual. She wasn't sending any of us back to school in a pāpa'a (cooked crisp) black state. She would scold us, "it's bad enough that you are kua'āina (from the country—countryfied) and "Kanaka" (she said this very derogatorily, the way the haole lunas, foremen on the plantations, said it), but to be pāpa'a, black, well, we can avoid that. We listened and heard her and stayed out of bathing suits and away from the beaches.

There were many times when I was young, that I wondered why she never wanted us girls to be pāpa'a, black—she allowed it for the boys, but never us! I thought, she has really not looked at us, especially Aineiki. When Aineiki was pāpa'a black by the summer sun, she was beautiful! Her tawny, blemishless, skin glowed. Her heavy lidded, black lashed, deeply-set eyes, laughed from out of her smooth, dark face which was always fringed with masses of shiny, too curly black hair. Her nose was Dad's, high bridged, straight and narrow, and her mouth was Mama's, full lipped and sensuous. And, when she circled her head with rings of pure white crownflowers and wore them in ropes around her neck and, donned a trimly fitted red holoku, and did the Mī Nei, she was beautiful!

When I was older and had gone away to school in Texas and had lived and travelled the continental U.S. for nearly four years, and had returned to my fair Hawai'i nei, I knew why Mama said, "it's bad enough that you are kua'āina and "Kanaka," but to be pāpa'a black, well, we can avoid that." I will never agree with her, but I will understand.

HINAHINA, 'ĀHINAHINA, 'UMI 'UMI O DOLE, SPANISH MOSS, DOLE'S BEARD, TILLANDSIA USNEOIDES

Soon after the Spanish moss was introduced in about 1920, the Hawaiians fashioned a lei from it. Because the plant reminded them of kauna'oa in texture, they used the same techniques to make the lei hinahina as was used for the lei kauna'oa.

Hinahina means gray or grayish. The Hawaiian gave this same name to other plants that were gray or grayish in appearance. Such plants as the silversword *(Argyroxiphium sandwicense)*, the native geraniums *(Geranium cunea-*

[29]From a song, PUA KALAUNU, by Alice Namakelua.

Fuchsias

Fuchsia lei

Canary bush lei

Wearing fuchsia and canary bush leis

Wearing strawflower leis

Strawflowers

Strawflower lei

(Opposite page, top left to right): Wearing the jade lei
(Opposite page, bottom left to right): Jade flowers; Vanda lei (maunaloa style); Vanda lei (a single style).
(Below, left): Vanda field & Vanda flower (right)

(Below, left to right): Vanda leis (maunaloa, double and mixed) with other leis & wearing the vanda lei

tum var. *tridens),* the native artemisia *(Artemisia australis)* and the native heliotrope *(Heliotropium anomalum* var. *argenteum)* were all called hinahina or ʻāhinahina. Another name given to the Spanish moss, ʻumiʻumi o Dole, means Dole's beard and received its name from the famous gray beard of Sanford B. Dole, first and only president of the Hawaiian Republic. In pageantry of recent years, the Spanish moss is almost always substituted for the native hinahina *(H. anomalum* var. *argenteum)* to represent the island of Kahoʻolawe, since it has become easier to get Spanish moss than it is to get the native heliotrope. Many native Hawaiians of modern times have never even seen the true lei hinahina of Kahoʻolawe.

The Spanish moss lei is made by using the lengths of moss as is; by twisting shorter lengths together to make a longer one; or by braiding short lengths to make a long enough braid to encircle the head or neck. It has an unusual appearance which is enhanced by dark hair and dark skin.

It was the first time that I had made the leis for my friend's fashion show. It was an assignment from the mayor's office. I had offered my services to my friend for other shows prior to this one, but he had never needed them. This show was going to be a big one! It was being staged especially for the wives of mayors from all over the country and from some of the Pacific nations. Richard, my friend, had planned and worked with a committee from the mayor's office and the work was finally handed to me. The plan called for eight island leis, and one red, one blue, one white, one yellow and one pink lei and one hat lei to be made in the wili or haku style. My assignment was the red, blue, white, yellow, and pink leis, the hat lei, and the lei hinahina for the island of Kahoʻolawe. The rest of the leis would come from the mayors of the other Hawaiian counties. They would send the lei of their islands. "Perfect!" I said, "Now all I need are two or three other lei makers and we'll have our part of the job done.

As the time for the show grew nearer, I received frantic telephone calls from the mayor's office. One caller said, "Marie, we received a letter from Maui, no one at Mr. Tam's office knows what the Maui rose or the lokelani is and they can't find anybody on Molokaʻi or Lānaʻi who knows how to make the lei kukui and the lei kaunaʻoa. What are we going to do? You know that this show has to be authentic and perfect." "I know," I said heaving a sigh and closing my eyes slowly. "We'll make those leis too." "Fine, but are you sure that you know what all these things are?" "Yes," another heaving sigh and closing of the eyes, "I know, this has to be authentic!"

The next day another frantic call! "The Kauaʻi mayor's office called, they say that the mokihana is not in season. What do we do?" "String up some other kind of green seed and make sure you say that it is a substitute, or, go without it because that is the only place where you can get it—we can't make that one." To myself I said, "this has got to be a conspiracy! I wonder if all these mayors get along?" Aloud I said, "now please don't call me and tell me that the Hawaiʻi mayor's office can't find lehua or somebody to make the lei lehua."

My crew of lei making experts, Akiko Nakamura, Betty Ikehara, Tomie Karasuda, sister Irma, daughter Roen and a novice, Bobbie Meheula, finally completed nine out of the fourteen leis needed for the show. I delivered them, unpacked them and laid them on the table with the lei kukui which had arrived earlier and was beautifully made, the substitute lei mokihana, the lei ʻilima, and the lei pupu OʻNiʻihau. As I unpacked, the lei lehua arrived—the mayor of Hawaiʻi County had come through. I could hear the models for the fashion show oh-ing and ah-ing and I turned to look at this lei that I knew was worth oh-ing about and my face dropped with disappointment. Someone was carrying a beautiful lei lehua haole (Calliandra inaequilatera) *and no one in the room knew the difference. I said nothing. "I'll tell Richard," I thought, and he can do what he will. Who is saying what about authenticity."*

I turned to finish the unpacking. The social director of the hotel came in. She viewed the leis and raved about them, "These are so-o-o-o beautiful! And what is this?" she asked pointing to a silvery gray-white lei. "Lei hinahina," I replied. "No that isn't the lei hinahina," she said with such authority. I could almost believe her if I didn't know any better. I shrugged my shoulders and made a slight grimace. "This is not the lei of Kaho'olawe," she went on. I shrugged my shoulders again and again I made a slight grimmace. I was tired and I had had enough problems with people knowing and mostly not knowing. I decided not to pursue the challenge, not to tell Richard about his lei lehua haole and go home, but through the door came a blue haired, distinguished, Hawaiian matron followed by Richard, who said, very loudly, when she saw the lei lehua haole "Auwē, Richard, somebody made a mistake. I hope you don't pass it off as the lei of Hawai'i." Everybody greeted her and I could see that she was one who commanded respect.

The social director beckoned to her to come over to the table. She came. "Aloha mai" she acknowledged me. I smiled. "How beautiful. My, this is the real hinahina. I've not seen this lei for many years. You know, everyone nowadays use the 'umi'umi-o-Dole." She made a stroking motion with her two hands from her chin to her stomach, then addressed me." 'He u'i maoli keia lei hinahina, he 'a'ala mau."

I think that it was then that I decided that the whole world should know about this lei and all the other beautiful ones. The lei had already inspired me. I had talked with and watched older leimakers. I had read accounts and stories of leis in library books and archive newspapers. I had sung songs about leis. I had acquired a knowledge of lei materials through constant use of them and had learned to identify them by Hawaiian, common, and botanical names. I knew where to find the materials in the wilds or growing in someone's garden. I had become proficient in all techniques of lei making through searching, questioning and practice. Each time I acquired a new skill, a fact, found a new, old plant or heard a new story, the excitement of discovery made me want to share it. This must be the way to keep a beautiful tradition going.

KUKUNA-O-KA-LĀ, MANGROVE, ORIENTAL MANGROVE, MANY PETALED MANGROVE, BRUGUIERA GYMNORHIZA

All mangroves have been introduced to Hawai'i, some in 1902 and the one that produced the material for the lei kukuna-o-ka-lā in 1922. The Hawaii Sugar Planters Association introduced it and ten years later, it had become naturalized at Heeia on O'ahu. Twenty years later, in 1952, there were many Hawaiians who had attached the title "traditional" to the lei kukuna-o-ka-lā. By then, the kukuna-o-ka-lā had established itself culturally as well as naturally in the Hawaiian environment.

The stiff yellow to red calyxes resembling the rays of the sun, (thus the Hawaiian name, kukuna-o-ka-lā) are gathered from trees that grow at the mouths of streams in brackish water during the later summer and through the fall when they are plentiful.

The calyxes are strung most often lengthwise through the center and occasionally crosswise through the ovary or stem. The lei kukuna-o-ka-lā looks like a golden yellow centipede and when dried to a nice brown, you have to look again to make sure that it isn't one.

One really doesn't appreciate the lei kukuna-o-ka-lā until he has gathered the calyxes for himself and has fought off the mosquitoes and sloshed knee deep in swamp mud and water. Appreciation increases when one discovers that lei kukuna-o-ka-lā will keep well for more than a week and is even wearable after it is completely dried.

p to bottom): Mixed leis. Asparagus, stephanotis calyxes and ovaries;
ugainvillea, Hilo holly, pūkiawe, tī, manuka, cockscomb and pala'ā fern
idendrum orchid, parasol flower, dusty miller and privet

(Top to bottom): Chrysanthemum, rose, and asparagus; Carnation and rose; Parasol flower, liko lehua, calendulas and pala'ā fern.

(Top to bottom): Chrysanthemum, statice, Peruvian Lily and fern
Globe amaranth, baby's breath, bougainvillea and dusty miller
Marigold, 'ōhi'a lehua and cockscomb

(Top to bottom): Dendrobium orchid, sweet alyssum, pansy, fuchsias, and palapalai fern
Dendrobium orchid, liko lehua, pūkiawe, geranium
Epidendrum orchid, 'ōhai ali'i, ixora, ōhi'a lehua, calendula and kīkā

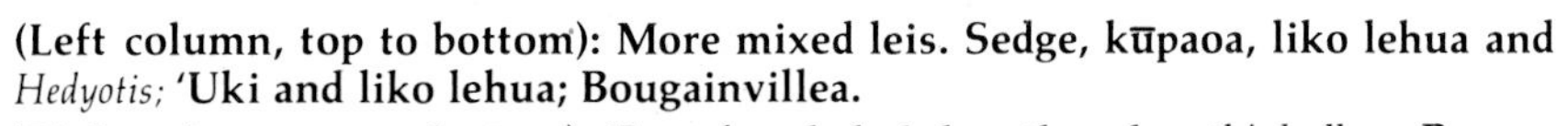
(Left column, top to bottom): More mixed leis. Sedge, kūpaoa, liko lehua and *Hedyotis;* **'Uki and liko lehua; Bougainvillea.**

(Right column, top to bottom): Feverfew, baby's breath and *spathiphyllum;* **Pansy, marguerite, cockscomb and fern; Cockscomb, pūkiawe, epidendrum orchid, and ageratum.**

(Left column, top to bottom): Lichen, pūkiawe, 'ōhi'a lehua; Rose, pūkiawe and palapalai fern; 'Ōhi'a lehua, rose, and statice.

(Right column, top to bottom): Baby's breath, statice, 'ōhi'a lehua, chrysanthemum, ageratum and pala'ā fern; Zinnia, cockscomb, moa, rose and palapalai fern; 'Ōhi'a lehua, *Erythrina* and fern.

ALAHE'E-HAOLE, WALAHE'E-HAOLE, MOCK ORANGE, MURRAYA PANICULATA

A native of India to the Philippines and the East Indies, the mock orange was "common in gardens" between 1865 and 1872 according to Hillebrand. The Hawaiians named it after the Alahe'e or Walahe'e, a native dry forest plant whose shiny green leaves resembled those of the mock orange. Although the mock orange may grow to a tree of great heights, islanders keep plants trimmed in hedges for homes, parks and other public places. The shiny, green, compound leaves are tied together using the wili method of lei construction.

The lei alahe'e-haole was probably an invention of a kumu hula and her student dancers who discovered during World War II that some lei materials were difficult to acquire since many of the mountain areas from which they came were off limits to civilians. They substituted and the result was the mock orange lei with shiny green leaves reminiscent of the maile in appearance, but not in scent. It sufficed. It filled the need of the kumu hula and her student dancer and has since become a lei that is preferred for its own beauty as often as it is used as a substitute for the lei maile.

CUP-AND-SAUCER PLANT, PARASOL FLOWER, COOLIE HAT FLOWER, HOLMSKIOLDIA SANGUINEA

Fairly recent introductions, the rust colored form in 1914, the lavendar-pink *(H. tettensis)* and lemon yellow forms in the mid 1900's, the flowers of the cup-and-saucer plants soon became materials for the lei maker. The rust colored calyxes when pierced and strung on fine, but strong thread reminded the Hawaiians of the rust lei 'ilima. Many hundred calyxes are needed for one strand and at least three strands made up on lei. The papery texture and long lasting quality, the rich color, the painstaking time and patience needed to string this lei, make it a highly prized possession. All colors, flowers and calyxes intact, are used in bunches in the lei wili.

PUKANAWILA, PUA KEPALŌ, BOUGAINVILLEA, BOUGAINVILLEA SPP.

The bougainvilleas, natives of South America, have been cultivated in Hawai'i since about 1827. *B. spectabilis* with purplish-red flowering bracts, and *B. glabra* with rose-red flowering bracts were the earliest introductions. Many other varieties were cultivated in other warm countries and were soon found in Hawai'i, brick-red, rust, pink, lavendar, yellowish, white and "double" forms. The bright colored, somewhat papery bracts which contained one or more inconspicuous cream colored flowers were pierced through the flat surface of the bracts and passed on to strong thread for the lei pukanawila. It requires many hundred flowering bracts to construct this lei which may be two to three inches in diameter and weigh less than a few ounces. Bougainvilleas are attached in bunches to a center cord with a binding thread and other flowers for a lei wili and are often sewn to a backing for a lei humu-papa.

Pua kepalō, devil's flower, is the name Kona Hawaiians give to the bougainvillea since the brilliant red, purple and orange flowers seem to resemble the fires of hell and the devil himself.

PUA-PEPA, STRAWFLOWER, EVERLASTING, HELICHRYSUM BRACTEATUM

The strawflower, an annual flowering plant native to Australia, is grown in many Hawaiian gardens especially for their long lasting, papery white, yellow, orange, red and pink flowers. The flowers are usually sewn to a backing, sometimes with other everlasting type flowers, for a lei humu-papa. Lei sellers who lined the docks at the turn of the century constructed their lei pua-pepa in this manner where they were usually purchased by local men and women for their hats. By the 1950s the lei pua-pepa (paper flower lei) gained renewed popularity when someone put them on lauhala hats which were the "in" thing to wear with the colorful mu'umu'us and aloha shirts. Today, Hawaiian cowboys may be seen wearing such leis on their hats.

Present day lei sellers will pierce the flowers through their centers and string them on sturdy string for the tourist who wants an everlasting lei.

VANDA 'MISS JOAQUIN', V. 'MISS AGNES JOAQUIM'

The vanda lei, as it is commonly called, is one of the two leis that made its debut at the islandwide lei contest in Honolulu. *Vanda* 'Miss Joaquim' first appeared in a lei created for the contest by some unknown person for Herbert Shipman, orchid grower from Hilo, in 1938. It won a second prize in the lavendar division. It appeared again in 1947 and 1950, two *Vanda* 'Miss Joaquim' leis made by Mrs. Woodrow Lee of Lunalilo Home Road won the grand prize. Each of the two leis were strung differently. In both leis the light lavendar petals of the vanda were removed leaving only the darker lavendar, yellow tinted center and broad fan-shaped lip. In one lei, these parts of the blossoms were strung through the spurs and the lips were arranged first one on the right and then one on the left or two on the right and two on the left. The pattern was repeated. The finished lei resembled the lavendar lei maunaloa *(Canavalia carthartica)* and because of this resemblence, today it is mistakenly called "maunaloa lei." In the second lei the parts of the blossoms were strung through the spurs again, but the lips were arranged all on one side of the lei. The first of these two methods of stringing the *Vanda* 'Miss Joaquim' is the most popular today. The vanda is also strung with all of its petals intact and is called the "single vanda lei." Sometimes the cast-a-way petals are strung together. Other times the light lavendar petals and the dark lavandar lip are all torn off and cast aside and only the centers are strung.

A "single" vanda lei is made by stringing the flowers, with all petals intact, longitudinally through their centers. Fifty orchids are needed to make a single lei.

Present day leimakers have devised a variety of stringing patterns by tearing the vanda blossoms apart (See illustration, plate 12, page 170) and have given them various exotic names in keeping with the tourist industry, and since they claim that the terms "single" and "double" are not explicit enough. Their names are sometimes confusing because they differ from island to island and from leimaker to leimaker. All, however, agree on the "maunaloa" vanda lei.

The *V.* 'Miss Joaquim' is a comparatively new introduction. It was first introduced in August 1930 by Lester "Bill" Bryan of Hilo. Bryan got twenty-four cuttings from the Singapore Botanical Gardens while on a plant collecting trip for the Hawaii Sugar Planters Association (HSPA). Only fifteen cuttings survived the trip.

Dr. Harold Lyon of HSPA introduced cuttings to O'ahu a few months later on his return from a world cruise.

This *Vanda* hybrid cross *(Vanda hookeriana* × *V. teres)* was made in about 1890 by a Mr. Joaquim of Singapore and named for his daughter Agnes. It became world famous only after orchid growers on the island of Hawai'i began to market it in 1946 on grand scale to department stores across the United States. A few Vanda leis were made, but it wasn't until Mrs. Woodrow Lee's Vanda leis appeared at the Honolulu Lei Day Show that leimakers and lei sellers the Islands over began to string the *Vanda 'Miss Joaquim'* into garlands for lei lovers the world over. Today, it is one of the more popular leis because it is well designed, and has good color. It is long lasting and the flowers are available all year round with large amounts in June, July, and August.

Hilo and Puna districts on the island of Hawai'i are the centers of the *Vanda* growing industry, though many "backyard growers" exist on all the islands.

The *Vanda* lei like the lei poni-mō'ī and lei pīkake are leis which are most often purchased from florists and lei sellers rather than made at home because great numbers of flowers are necessary or special growing conditions are needed to produce the great number of flowers needed for one lei.

Although the kui method is the usual one to make this lei, sometimes vandas are used with other materials in the lei wili.

Other vandas are used in leis as well as other members of the large orchid family. Of all the many orchids that are used today, none of them are native to Hawai'i. Most were introduced from tropical America, Asia, Malaysia, Australia, and the Pacific Islands during the last few years of the Nineteenth Century and the first thirty years of the Twentieth Century. Many were crossed creating new hybrids. The four native orchids are too rare and too inconspicuous for lei making.

Commonly used orchids, especially on the island of Hawai'i are: dendrobiums (one of them being *D. anosmum,* the honohono orchid); epidendrums, *Phaius tankervilliae* (the brown Chinese ground orchid), *Spathoglottis, Oncidiums, Phalaenopsis* and *Arundina bambusifolia* (the wild bamboo orchid).

JADE VINE, STRONGYLODON MACROBOTRYS

One of the most recently introduced temporary lei material, the jade vine, a native of the Philippines came to Hawai'i in the form of two plants in 1950. Earlier efforts to introduce the seeds or plants of the jade vine failed. Robert and John Allerton brought the plants from Los Baños Government Nursery in February, 1950. They gave one to Foster Gardens and kept the other one. Their plant died, but the one at Foster Gardens thrived and went unnoticed for about five years until 1955 when Lorraine Kuck then put together an arrangement of a dozen or more inflorescences for a dedication of a building at Foster Garden. People became very excited about the jade vine, so Dr. Harold Lyon and Colin Potter made a series of airlayers and began to distribute them.

The following year, 1956, many more people became excited with the jade vine when they viewed for the first time a jade lei. This spectacular lei was presented at the Lei Day Contest in Honolulu where it won the grand prize. The lei maker was Betty Lou Ho. Mrs. Ho used the kui method of lei making for this first jade lei. Five flowers were strung together by piercing them laterally just above the ovaries, then the thread ends were tied together drawing the flowers into a circlet. Each circlet was then strung through the center onto a thick cord. About two hundred blossoms were used.

In 1957 the jade lei again took top honors at the Lei Day Contest. To show the versatility of the blossoms, Mrs. Ho strung them to create another design. The designs created during these contests are those that are used most frequently by leimakers today.

The jade vine begins it blooming season as early as February and often continues to bloom through June.

My friend Betty Ho is a vital, creative, clever, aware and often outspoken person. We have known each other since our days at Kamehameha and we've much in common. We are both art oriented and art trained. We've worked together and have held the same positions with the Department of Parks and Recreation of the City and County of Honolulu, first as recreation directors and later as the art specialist. We've climbed mountains and explored valleys together. We've haunted every plant nursery on the island of O'ahu and some on the other islands too. We've thrown ceramic pots, made batiks, invented Christmas tree ornaments, and stitched on Hawaiian quilts

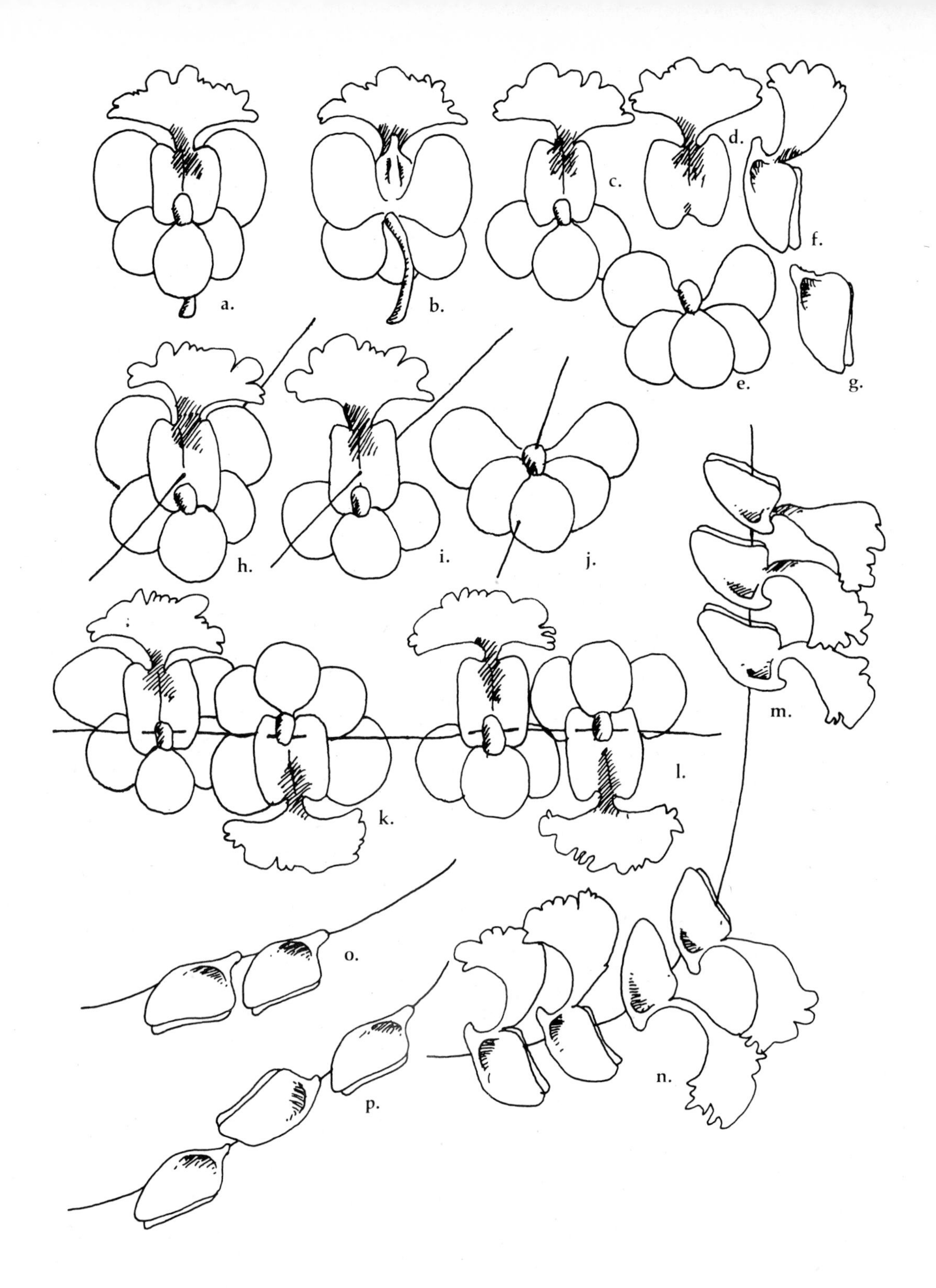

PLATE 12. THE VERSATILE VANDA. VARIOUS TORN APART PIECES AND STRINGING PATTERNS.

- a. front view
- b. back view
- c. two pale lavendar petals removed
- d. front view lip and cup only
- e. detached (five) petals and stamen
- f. side view of lip and cup
- g. cup only
- h. kui pololei, entire blossoms (a.)
- i. kui pololei, two petals removed (c.)
- j. kui pololei, petals and stamen (e.)
- k. kui lau, entire blossoms, stems removed (a.)
- l. kui lau, two petals removed from blossoms (c.)
- m. kui pololei, lip and cup (f.)
- n. kui lau, lip and cup alternating from side to side by sets of two (f.)
- o. kui pololei, cups (g.)
- p. kui lau, cups alternating from side to side (g.)

together. We've shopped in far away bazaars, shops, alleyways, artists' studios, and department stores. We've designed magnificent exhibits for ethno-botany, Chinese brush painting, and Easter egg shows. We've agreed on a lot of things and have disagreed on as many. We have both been fascinated by our Hawaiian heritage, our art, and our leis.

When did this fascination begin? I'm not sure, but along the way, we made leis together and Betty's acute awareness of things about her helped her to make a little dent in the cultural history of Hawai'i. She received permission and had gathered from Foster Garden the then little known blue-green jade vine flowers, and with them she created the first jade vine lei in the history of Hawai'i and probably the world. It won the Mayor's Grand Prize at the Lei Contest at Honolulu in 1956 and another jade vine lei designed differently and made by Betty for use on a hat won that same prize the following year.

We continued to make leis for the Lei Contest while Betty's husband, Ray, checked on us, teased us, fed us while we were making them, then puffed up with pride with us when we won. My husband watched our children, thought we were a little crazy, then did as Ray did when we won. In 1958 and 1959 we won division awards but not the coveted Mayor's Grand Prize, but in 1960, my turn came and my lei of mixed purple flowers, lantana, globe amaranth, statice, and jacaranda buds won it for our team of McDonald-Ho. If you've ever won the Pulitzer or Nobel Prize or an Oscar or a Gold Medal at the Olympics or the baseball game in the sandlot, then you will know the feeling of reward, accomplishment, success, and pride in one's self that you enjoy at the moment when you know that you've won.

1960 was our last year in the Lei Contest. The revised rules disallowed employees of the Department of Parks and Recreation. We continued to help in the staging of the contest and some of our proteges became the winners. Then Betty and Ray went to live in Hong Kong and Betty became a designer, manufacturer, exporter-importer, wholesaler and retailer of plastic goods among them plastic leis and some said, "auwē nō ho'i ē!"

OTHER TEMPORARY MATERIALS

The lei making techniques of the ancient Hawaiians made it possible for any and all materials to be used for necklaces or crowns. The list of fresh, natural materials is endless. These are some.

Kulapepeiao, *Fuchsia magellanica.*
Candle bush, *Cassia alata.*
Ha'ikū, Kahiliflower, *Grevillea banksii.*
Huapala, *Pyrostegia venustra.*
Koniaka, China aster, *Callistephus chinensis.*
Lanalana, ylang ylang, *Cananga odorata.*
Mikilana, Mei-sui-lan, Chinese rice flower, *Aglaia odorata.*
Miulana melemele, orange champak, *Michelia champaca.*
Miulana ke'oke'o, pak lan, white champak, *Michelia alba.*
Pōpō lehua, *Ixora casei.*
Pua-hoku-hihi, wax plant, *Hoya bicarinata.*
Lepe-a-moa, cockscomb, *Celosia argentea* var. *cristata.*
Shrimp plant, *Beloperone guttata.*
White shrimp plant, *Nicoteba betonica.*
Wiliwili haole, *Erythrina orientalis.*
Downy myrtle, *Rhodomyrtus tomentosa.*
Jacaranda, *Jacaranda acutifolia.*
Gold tree, prima vera, *Tabebuia donnell-smithii.*
Pink tecoma, *Tabebuia pentaphylla.*
Butterfly pea, *Clitoria ternata.*
Honekakala, honeysuckle, *Lonicera japonica.*
Lantana, *Lantana camara.*
Sandpaper vine, *Petrea volubilis.*
Paka, tobacco, *Nicotiana tabacum.*
Browallia, *Browallia* spp.
Pīanuhea, pī wai anuhea, sweet pea, *Lythrus odoratus.*
Lady of the night, *Brunfelsia americana.*
Yesterday-today-tomorrow, *Brunfelsia latifolia.*

Snapdragon, *Antirrhinum majus.*
Coral plant, *Russelia equisetiformis.*
Balloon flower, Chinese bellflower, *Platycodon grandiflorum.*
'Uki haole, gladiola, *Gladiolus* spp.
Bellflower, *Campanula* sp.
Edging lobelia, *Lobelia erinus.*

DAISY OR SUNFLOWER FAMILY

Calendula, Helianthus, Helenium, Gazania, Gerbera, Bellis, Dimorphoteca, Wedelia, Tagetes (marigolds), *Coreopsis, Zinnia, Cosmos, Dahlia, Chrysanthemum, Gaillardia, Rudbeckia, Stokesia, Aster, Achillea* (yarrow), *Matricaria* (feverfew), *Ageratum, Centaurea* (cornflower, bachelor's buttons).

'Ahu'awa, *Cyperus javanicus, C. hypochlorus.*
'Ahu'awa haole, *Cyperus alternifolius.*
Delphinium.
Candytuft, *Iberis umbellata.*
Galphimia gracilis
Heather, *Erica subdivaricata.*
False heather, *Cuphea hyssopifolia.*
Hilo holly, hen's eyes, *Ardisia crispa.*
Mexican indigo, *Jacobina spicigera.*
Manuka, tea tree, *Leptospermum* spp.
Stock, gilliflower, *Matthiola* spp.
Pentas, *Pentas lanceolata.*
Beard tongue, *Penstemon.*
Baby's breath, *Gypsophila paniculata.*
Statice, sea lavendar, *Limonium.*
Begonia spp.

Ho'ohihi wale au i kou nani
Ku'u pua ylang-ylang onaona
Kui ia lei ho'ohie
Uluwehi ulu mahiehie.
Na ke ahe makani i lawe mai
Ko 'ala onaona i o'u nei
Me he ala e'i mai ana
E na kaua e ke hoa.[30]

I admire your beauty
My fragrant ylang-ylang flower
I will fashion a lei
So decorative and beautiful.
Your fragrance is brought to me
By the gentle wind
It seems to be the soft whisper of a lover
Calling, "come be with me."

HOW TO CARE FOR LEIS

Through the years various ways of caring for permanent and temporary leis have been developed, but it seems that the best are still the ways of the ancient Hawaiians. The permanent leis are still best stored in moisture free containers wrapped in some soft nonabrasive material, with some tobacco to ward off the insects. Seed leis need special handling if the nut meat has not been entirely removed. They should be stored in separate containers and re-strung and re-buffed each year until the nut meat has all decayed or has been eaten away by insects. Some lei owners recommend moth balls and camphor to keep insects away. The lei palaoa, the lei hulu manu, the lei pūpū and the lei hua should have the same care as other fine jewelry.

The care of temporary leis is not so general though one needs to remember that these leis are not meant to last forever. They are momentary. They are temporary. The thought that accompanies the gift of the lei will live forever, but the gift itself will die and must be allowed to die. Therein lies the true beauty of these wondrous creations. As short-lived as they are, they still need some care and there will be times when they need to be stored over a night or two.

The best way to keep temporary leis fresh is the ancient way, sprinkle with a little water, gently shake the excess off, wrap in a pū'olo lā'ī or place in a hā mai'a, and keep in a cool shaded place. Since the pū'olo lā'ī or the hā mai'a are not that readily available particularly in our urban areas, the second best way is to wrap the leis in damp newspaper and store in the refrigerator or some cool shaded place.

[30]From a song, KU'U PUA YLANG-YLANG, by John K. Almeida, 1953.

Some flowers do not take too kindly to too much water. These should be sprinkled sparingly or not at all because they bruise easily. White flowers and some of the delicate yellow flowers fall in this group. Pīkake, gardenia, yellow and white ginger, tuberose, freesia, crownflower, plumeria and puakenikeni leis should be wrapped in damp newspaper and stored in the refrigerator. All of these leis can be strung the evening before they are to be used and allowed to lay out on the lawn in the cool Hawaiian night air where they will keep well.

Vandas should be sprinkled lightly, stored in a box with a newspaper lining in the refrigerator. If bundled too tightly without space to breathe, they will turn white.

Fern and foliage leis, such as, pala'ā, palapalai, maile, alahe'e haole, need not be refrigerated. They may be wrapped in a damp cloth and kept in a cool shaded place. If they are refrigerated, they should be wrapped in damp newpaper.

The highly prized lei 'ilima lasts for only a few hours. If strung the night before for use the next day, it should be stored in a paper-lined box or covered plastic container without water.

Carnations and pakalana can be submerged in water for a little while then removed and all the water shaken free, then wrapped in newspaper and refrigerated. All other fresh leis are simply wrapped in damp newspaper and refrigerated if they need to last for two or more days. If they need to last for a day or less, just sprinkle with water or place on damp newpaper or a damp cloth, keep in a cool shaded place like the kitchen sink, the bathtub, the laundry tub, or a shaded spot on the patio or in the yard.

All paper-wrapped bundles of leis may or may not be placed in a plastic bag for storage in the refrigerator.

I cringe every time someone asks me to make a fresh flower lei that will last until a week from this Tuesday, or when someone says, "I just got these 'ilima leis at a surprise birthday luncheon for me today, please tell me how to keep them so that I can wear them when I go to New York next week." Or, "I was so thrilled when my husband gave me this beautiful lei. Tell me how to keep it nice until next Saturday so I can wear it to my club meeting."

I shake my head and say to myself, "typically contemporary—"the value is not in the giving and the receiving, but in getting full use and the money's worth. I once advised a person to bronze it, or if that was too costly, then try freezing it. No sooner had I said it, I wanted to bite my tongue for I was doing what I had asked others not to do. I was ridiculing—my you're ignorant! This is a temporary lei of fresh natural materials. It can't last forever and a week from this Tuesday is forever for a temporary lei of fresh, natural materials. And, don't you know that it is the intangible that you take to New York with you and allow the tangible to serve its purpose, then change or die because it must. And this lei, this love, is for now. It is between you and him. Besides next week he may tell you he loves you with an "I love you" card or a vacuum cleaner. Why must visual beauty last forever? What is wrong with short-lived beauty? Is it less beautiful than any other kind of beauty?

LEIS TO HANDLE WITH CARE

As has been previously mentioned, very few materials escaped the leimaker's hands. Even plants that are poisonous or somewhat poisonous to humans if taken internally were and are still used for leis. The fragrant oleander *(Nerium oleander)* with single or double white, pink, coral and red flowers and the yellow tubular flowers of the be-still tree or yellow oleander, *(Thevetia peruviana)* were often strung into leis until Hawaiians discovered how poisonous the plants were. Princess Ruth wore leis of pink oleander without any ill effects. Some people will still wear the lei 'oliwa ('oliana of 'oleana) on their hats today, but it is not recommended for use.

Other more or less poisonous lei materials are the crownflower, pua kalaunu, *Calotropis gigantea;* the plumeria, melia, frangipani *Plumeria* spp.; the kīkanīa, *Solanum aculeatissimum;* the rosary-pea, black-eyed Susan, bead vine, the pūkiawe-lei, *Abrus precatorius;* the castor bean, castor oil plant, kolī, pā'aila, lā'au-'aila, *Ricinus communis;* the kahili flower, *Grevillea banksii.*

The Ko'olaus are still beautiful, I observed as I stood in the driveway garden of Irma and Walla's Kāne'ohe home. From the windward side of O'ahu this accordian pleated, yellow-green, blue-purple range of mountains had not changed since I left this place almost five years before to live in Waimea. Irma was gathering flowers for some leis, and I thought, as I exclaimed about the unchanging beauty of the mountains: I hope that the sprawling city and increasing population never infringes upon or mars the beauty of those mountain cliffs.

Now, why did I expect them to change? It hasn't been that long and that is a lot of mountain to bulldoze. Almost as if reading my mind, Irma said, "They will always be there, Marie." "What?" I questioned, not believing that she had read my thoughts, "the Ko'olaus" she replied. Yeah, I thought again, as long as there are people like you and me who are encouraged by the wonders of nature, who can gather parts of its beauty with care and respect as you are doing at this moment, then create another wondrous thing, there will always be the Ko'olau mountains.

I picked up some shears to help and the wanderings of my mind continued. I was reminded of the two of us and Jo when as children we gathered hibiscus leaves, then sat in the shade and carefully made hibiscus leaf leis for head and neck. There was nothing else for us to use. We connected the leaves together by overlapping tip and base ends then pinned them together with the detached stems forming a kind of chain. I smiled to myself and thought how ingenious we were!

We were not the only resourceful people for at about the same time in Puakō on Hawai'i lived a family involved in beekeeping. On occasions when a lei was needed at school, the mother collected kiawe (algaroba) blossoms and wove them into leis.

I thought, so instilled in us all is the tradition of giving and receiving a lei, that it is much like the Ko'olau mountains. It will always be.

My recollections of how the lei has influenced my life are not unique stories. Anyone who has been born or has grown up or has come to live in Hawai'i is influenced by the lei in much the same manner as I and can probably tell countless more stories. And this is the real significance of the lei. It has universal appeal. It will survive any and all cultural change, for there will always be people who will enjoy and need its beauty to express regard for others and self.

PAU

BIBLIOGRAPHY

BECKWITH, Martha. *Hawaiian Mythology*. University of Hawaii Press, 1970.

BIRD, Isabella Lucy. *Six months in the Sandwich Islands*. John Murray, London, 1890.

BROWN, Elizabeth D.W. *Polynesian Leis*. American Anthropologist Vol. 33 No. 4, Oct.-Dec., 1931.

BUCK, Peter H. (Te Rangi Hiroa). *Arts and Crafts of Hawaii*. Bishop Museum Press, 1957.

CARLQUIST, Sherwin. *A Natural History of Hawaii*. The Natural History Press. Garden City, New York, 1970.

DEGNER, Otto. *Plants Hawaii National Park*, Honolulu Star-Bulletin 1930. *Flora Hawaiiensis*, Books 1–4, 1946, Book 5, 1946–1957, Book 6, 1957–1963.

EDMUNDSON, Charles Howard. *Reef and Shore Fauna of Hawaii*, Bernice P. Bishop Museum, Special Publication 22, 1946.

ELBERT, Samuel H. and MAHOE, Noelani. *Na Mele o Hawai'i*, University of Hawaii Press, 1970.

ELLIS, William, Dr. *Narrative of a tour through Hawaii*. London, 1827.

EMERSON, Nathaniel B. *Unwritten Literature of Hawaii:* Bureau of American Ethnology Bul. 38, Washington, D.C., 1909.

EMERSON, Nathaniel B. *The Myth of Pele and Hiiaka*. Honolulu Star Bulletin, Ltd., 1915.

FORNANDER, Abraham, *An account of the Polynesian Race, Its Origins and Migrations*, Charles E. Tuttle Co., Japan, 1969.

HANDY, E.S. CRAIGHILL, EMORY, Kenneth P. and others. *Ancient Hawaiian Civilization*, Charles E. Tuttle Co., 1965.

HANDY, E.S. CRAIGHILL and HANDY, Elizabeth Green. *Native Planters in Hawaii. Their Life, Lore and Environment*. Bishop Museum Press, 1972.

HILLEBRAND, William F. *Flora of the Hawaiian Islands*, Heidelberg, 1888.

KAMAKAU, Samuel M. Translated by Mary Kawena Pukui. *Ka Po'e Kahiko, The People of Old*, Bishop Museum Press, 1964. Ruling Chiefs of Hawai'i. The Kamehameha Schools Press, 1961.

KELLY, JR., John M. *Folk Songs Hawaii Sings*. Charles Tuttle Company, Inc. Tokyo, Japan, 1963.

KING, Charles E. *King's Book of Hawaiian Melodies*. Honolulu, Hawaii, 1943, 1948.

KING, Charles E. *King's Songs of Hawai'i*. Honolulu, Hawaii, 1950.

KUCK, Lorraine E. *The Story of the Lei*. Tongg Publishing Company, Ltd., Honolulu, Hawaii, 1961.

MALO, David. Translated by Nathaniel B. Emerson. *Hawaiian Antiquities*. Bishop Museum Press, 1898.

NEAL, Marie C. *In Gardens of Hawai'i*. Bishop Museum Press, 1965.

NOBLE, Johnny. *Johnny Noble's Royal Collection of Hawaiian Songs*. Miller Music, Inc., New York, N.Y., 1929.

PUKUI, Mary Kawena, ELBERT, Samuel H. *Hawaiian Dictionary*. University of Hawaii Press, 1971.

STEWARD, C.S. *Journal of a Residence in the Sandwich Islands During the Years 1823, 1824, 1825*. University of Hawaii Press, 1970.

INDEX

D.

E.

F.

G.

H.

I.

J.

K.

L.

M.

N.

O.

P.

Q.

R.

S.

T.

U.

V.

W.

Y.

Z.